People of Destiny

A Humanities Series

9742

There comes a time,
we know not when,
that marks
the destiny of men.

Joseph Addison Alexander

People of Destiny

ROBERT FROST

By Norman Richards

*Grateful acknowledgment is here made
to Lawrance Thompson, official biographer
of Robert Frost, for his reading of this
manuscript and his suggestions for revision.*

CHILDRENS PRESS, CHICAGO

*The editors wish to express
their appreciation to Mr. Meyer Goldberg,
who created the series and inspired
the publication of* People of Destiny.

Cover and body design: John Hollis

Project editor: Joan Downing

---

*Illustrations: Robert O'Malley and
Ron Kangles—Hollis Associates*

Research editor: Robert Hendrickson

---

*Photographs: From the files of Wide World
Photos, Inc., The Bettmann Archive, the
University of Oklahoma Press, and the Jones
Library, Inc.*

Typesetting: American Typesetting Co.

Printing: Regensteiner Press

Contents

America Honors a Poet

January 20, 1961, was a day that belonged to statesmen and politicians rather than to poets. A new, young President, John F. Kennedy, was being inaugurated and the attention of the United States—and indeed, of the whole world—was focused on Washington, D.C. Millions of people watched their television sets as the inauguration ceremonies took place in front of the Capitol building.

One of the worst snowstorms in Washington's history had buffeted the area for more than twenty-four hours, and the ground was covered with deep snow. But Inauguration Day dawned clear and cold, with a gleaming landscape reflecting the sun's bright rays. Officials and bystanders turned their collars up to ward off the biting wind as they waited for the ceremonies to begin. A huge crowd had gathered in front of the official platform. Many people had stood for two hours, stamping their feet to avoid numbness.

Outgoing President Dwight D. Eisenhower and his wife had taken the traditional ride to the Capitol from the White House with the new President and his lovely, vivacious wife. They sat on the platform along with outgoing Vice-President Richard Nixon, newly elected Vice-President Lyndon Johnson, former President Harry S. Truman, Congressional leaders, and other officials.

After the singing of the national anthem and religious observances, an elderly, white-haired man was introduced as "Robert Frost, our national poet." He needed little additional introduction, for almost everyone knew who Robert Frost was—even those who did not read poetry. Over the years he had won four Pulitzer Prizes for poetry and many national awards and honorary degrees. Twice the United States Senate had passed resolutions honoring him on his birthday.

Frost walked in halting steps to the microphone, a slightly stooped man in his middle eighties with a body that looked as if it had once been rugged and powerful. His familiar shock of snow-white, unruly hair was blown by the wind but his face wore the kindly, serene expression that the public had come to know.

Most people there that day did not realize that Robert Frost was far from being a simple country poet. He was a complex, sensitive, deep-thinking artist who had struggled against—and hated—tremendous adversity, years of obscurity, and personal tragedy. His place as America's most honored and popular poet had not been attained easily.

President-elect John F. Kennedy had long admired Frost's poetry, and Frost, in turn, had been impressed with the remarkable young man from Massachusetts as he watched him rise in national politics. Kennedy's eloquent speeches often contained quotations from Frost's work. The poet had publicly predicted Kennedy's election to the presidency, and out of admiration and gratitude the young statesman had asked him to take part in the inauguration ceremonies.

This portrait of Robert Frost was taken shortly before the inauguration ceremonies of President John F. Kennedy in 1961.

Wide World Photos

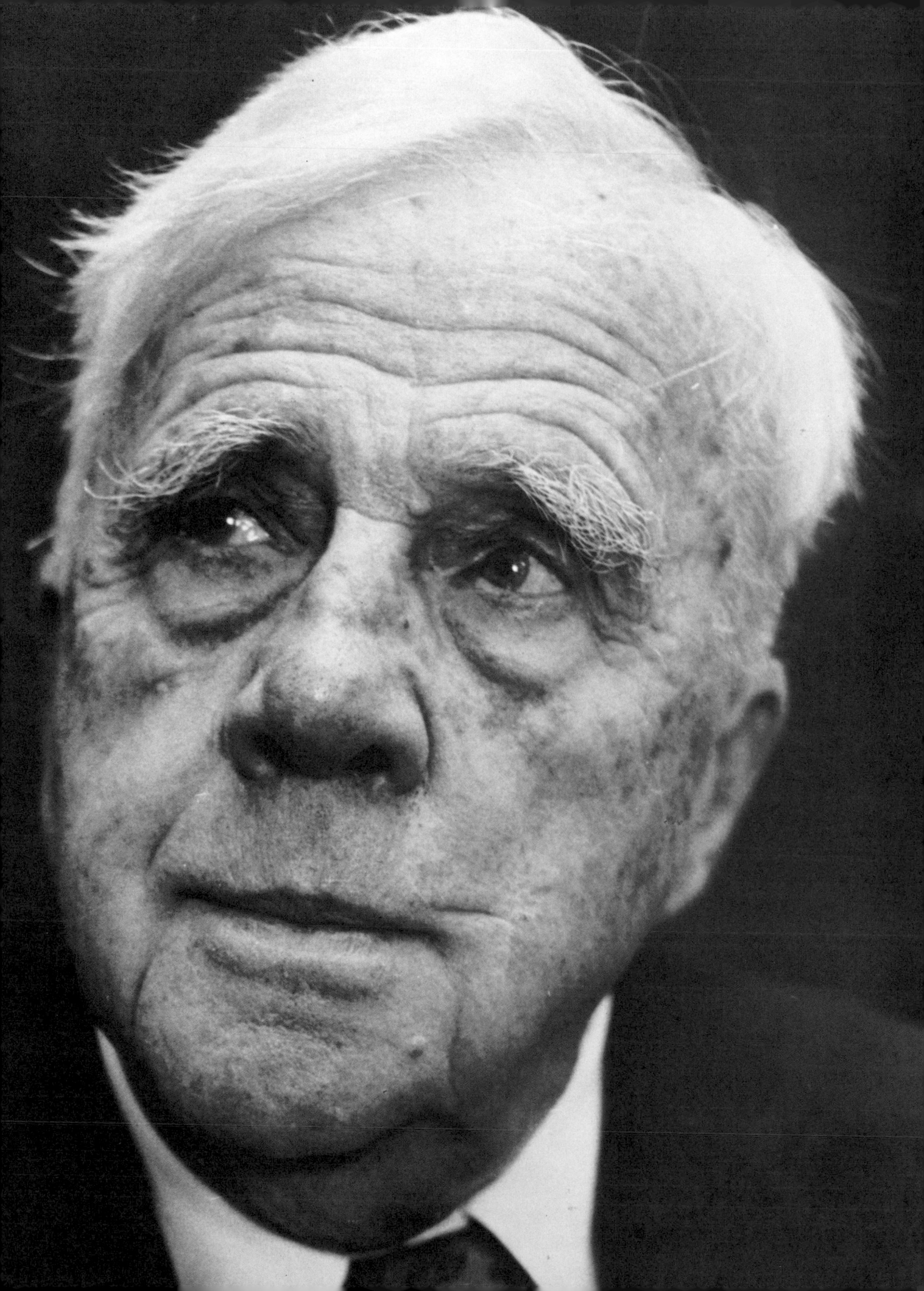

Frost was pleased to accept, not so much for himself, he told Kennedy, but for the cause of the arts and literature. Never before had a poet been invited to take part in the inauguration of a president. Extending this invitation was the first of many acts by John F. Kennedy that were designed to give full recognition to the arts as a vital part of American life.

When Frost was asked to read an appropriate poem from the great body of work he had amassed over the years, he asked if the President-elect had a particular choice. Kennedy chose one that had been composed many years earlier, entitled "The Gift Outright." It was a short, unrhymed, metered poem that expressed a deep feeling for America in Frost's typical conversational language. Besides reading this as the official inaugural poem, the poet decided to compose some verse as an introduction to it.

As he stood behind the lectern, he squinted in the glare of sun and snow and tried to read the verses he had composed. But the wind kept blowing the pages and he couldn't see well enough to read aloud after he began. He halted, tried again, and halted once more. The sun was just too blinding.

The crowd's sympathy went out to the elderly man and warm applause followed. He seemed to take heart at this and he told them that the verse was merely to have been a preface to a poem he did not have to read. Then he threw his shoulders back and began to recite "The Gift Outright" from memory in a clear, resonant voice.

Eighty-five-year-old poet Robert Frost has trouble reading a preface to a poem during inaugural ceremonies. A hat shading his written words didn't help.

THE GIFT OUTRIGHT

The land was ours before we were the land's.
She was our land more than a hundred years
Before we were her people. She was ours
In Massachusetts, in Virginia,
But we were England's, still colonials,
Possessing what we still were unpossessed by,
Possessed by what we now no more possessed.
Something we were withholding made us weak
Until we found out that it was ourselves
We were withholding from our land of living,
And forthwith found salvation in surrender.
Such as we were we gave ourselves outright
(The deed of gift was many deeds of war)
To the land vaguely realizing westward,
But still unstoried, artless, unenhanced,
Such as she was, such as she would become.

Like the work of most great poets, the more this poem is read or heard, the clearer the meaning becomes. Frost was saying that America did not become great, even though her ancestors had lived here a long time, until Americans began to think of themselves as natives of their own great nation—a nation with its own traditions and culture. No longer were they mere offshoots of European civilization, living in the New World. They *belonged* to America; they were *of* America. When Americans gave themselves in spirit to the land where they lived, it stopped being just land and became a country with a national consciousness. The poem also showed the difference between selfish possession and the willingness of citizens to sacrifice for their country, including giving their lives to defend it. "(The deed of gift was many deeds of war.)"

The years seemed to fall away as Robert Frost recited his words triumphantly in the cold air. His vigor and strength seemed to symbolize the country he had always written about with deep feeling. He finished abruptly, applause ringing in his ears as he turned and walked to his seat.

Few would dispute the description of him as a national poet—a man in whom Americans could take pride. His reputation was as great or greater in other countries than it was in his homeland. But now the world could see that America recognized the national importance of the arts and the greatness of the poet chosen to represent them.

Heritage of Adventure

Robert Frost was a true "New England" poet. He captured in his poetry the peculiar speech of country people in that region as few others have. Though he was born and spent the first decade of his life in San Francisco, at the opposite end of the country, he had a valid claim to being a New Englander.

Ten generations of Frosts had lived in New England, beginning with the rugged pioneers who cleared the land in early colonial days. They were conservative, small-town people rooted in the Puritan tradition: churchgoing, thrifty, respectable, middle-class people. All except one, that is—Robert Frost's father, William Prescott Frost, Jr.

The son of a mill overseer in Lawrence, Massachusetts, William Frost was a restless, handsome youth with more than the usual penchant for "sowing a few wild oats" during his high school and college days. But he was very intelligent and he graduated from Harvard College *cum laude*, with a Phi Beta Kappa key. Full of contrariness, he had wanted to quit college during the Civil War and enlist in the Confederate Army, even though his family and friends were supporting the Union cause. His parents had managed to prevent this, and they hoped that he would mature before long and enjoy a brilliant future in the business world.

But he disappointed them again shortly after his graduation by refusing to accept a management-level job in a mill. Not content to fit neatly into the pattern of his family tradition, he wanted to take the plunge and seek his fortune in the Far West. He wanted to be a newspaperman, and the best place to pursue a career in journalism, he felt, was in the fast-growing new areas of the West. Characteristically,

Robert Frost's ancestors were rugged colonial pioneers who cleared the stony New England land for their farms.

he didn't think about it long but started for California.

Apparently he hadn't thought about it long enough to consider what the trip might cost him, for he soon ran short of funds. In Lewistown, Pennsylvania, he paused to take a job for awhile —one that he had heard about through Harvard contacts. He became principal of a small academy for one school year. The school authorities were impressed with the scholastic record of the good-looking young man, and they had no way of knowing about his wild habits of drinking, gambling, and charming the ladies.

The only other teacher on the staff was Isabelle Moodie, a lovely young Scottish girl with beautiful dark brown eyes and a trace of a burr in her voice. She had been raised in her uncle's home in Columbus, Ohio, to which she had been brought to live when she was twelve.

Isabelle had known tragedy long before she reached Columbus and the comfort and protection of her well-to-do uncle. Born in a seacoast town in Scotland, she was the daughter of an impetuous, romantic sea captain who went down with his ship in a fierce storm when she was only eight years old. Her mother disappeared and Isabelle had been taken in by her father's devout Presbyterian parents. After her grandfather's death she was sent to live with her uncle in America.

Her strict Presbyterian upbringing had made her deeply religious. But beneath her proper demeanor, she was a romantic, loving poetry and having some of her father's love of adventure.

It was natural that she would be attracted to the brilliant, brash, romantic William Frost, who talked of his plans to find adventure in the West. Isabelle was six years older than the dashing young principal, but his intelligence and confidence seemed to narrow the gap. He had always had an eye for beauty, but this girl was like no other he had known.

It was a whirlwind courtship, hindered only by his lack of religious belief, which worried her. But she thought she might influence him as time went by, and that he might find a religious belief. She accepted his formal proposal and they were married in Lewistown before the school year was finished.

In June of 1873, Isabelle and William resigned their positions and the new Mrs. Frost went to stay with her relatives in Columbus while her husband headed West to find a job.

Booming, raucous San Francisco attracted William Frost more than any other place, and he lost no time in getting there. Just as he had hoped, there were many job opportunities in the fast-growing city. He took a job as a reporter on the *Bulletin*, one of the leading newspapers, and then sent for his bride.

*The booming frontier town of San Francisco
as it looked in 1873 when Robert Frost's
adventurous father, William, went there to
look for work on a newspaper.*

For once, adventurous William Frost found the excitement he craved. The heyday of the Wild West was at its peak in the 1870's, and San Francisco was one of the wildest cities of all. To be sure, it had become more orderly since the gold rush days of a few decades earlier, and vigilante committees were no longer needed to do the bulk of law enforcement. But San Francisco was becoming the Queen City of the West—the headquarters of mining millionaires, railroad and shipping firms, and just about every type of get-rich-quick speculator imaginable. It was a booming seaport, a smuggler's haven, and a center of trade with the Orient.

Sailing ships filled the harbor and fishing boats unloaded their catch at the docks every day. Three- and four-story buildings of stone and stucco had replaced the wooden shacks of earlier years in the business district. Downtown, broad streets, some of them paved, were lined with board sidewalks. There were many saloons, restaurants, theaters, and churches in the city. Away from the waterfront, houses sprouted as the city expanded.

Frost had arrived from the East on the Union Pacific Railroad, which had been completed a few years before. It covered vast distances in the West, where buffalo and Indians still roamed.

The United States was united once again after the Civil War, and the de-

feated Confederate states were in difficult economic straits. Men were moving West by the thousands, to raise cattle and sheep; to work as miners, cowboys, blacksmiths, and railroad laborers; and to go into retail businesses in newly established communities.

America was an exciting, growing nation, and millions of immigrants from Europe were moving in to take advantage of the opportunities. Germany was emerging as a powerful nation and Queen Victoria was leading the British Empire through its greatest period of expansion. Africa was being carved up among the European powers, who claimed vast amounts of territory as colonies. But no nation was growing faster than America, which leaped ahead in industry and agriculture while offering the average man better opportunities than any other place on earth.

When Isabelle Moodie Frost arrived in San Francisco to join her husband, she was somewhat shocked at the uncivilized atmosphere of the city. The gracious ways of the Middle West and of her native land, Scotland, were not yet noticeable in this raw frontier city.

Miners, seamen, and business owners spent night after night gambling and drinking, and the streets weren't safe for a woman alone after dark.

Isabelle was determined to make the best of it, but there were many difficulties. For one thing, she hated housekeeping and preferred reading poetry to making an attractive home. William Frost was not much help to her. He was intrigued by the people he met as a newspaper reporter and quickly became involved in politics, the stock market, and gambling. He seldom came home in the evenings. They moved often, living in apartments or hotels, and never settled down long enough to feel they had a real home.

It was in this environment that their son was born and raised during his early years. Both parents were delighted at the birth of the boy, whom William Frost decided to name Robert Lee to demonstrate his stubborn Confederate sympathies. "Robbie," as he was called, entered the world on March 26, 1874—a world of excitement, violence, and tragedy that he was destined to experience in full measure.

William Frost's bride, Isabelle, was uneasy in the wild town of San Francisco where street scenes like this one were not uncommon. She soon learned to stay at home after dark.

Boyhood by the Bay

San Francisco was a colorful, intriguing place for young Robert Lee Frost. The sounds of foreign voices down on the docks, lusty masculine laughter in the streets, and the clanging bells of the new cable cars on the steep hills mingled with the muffled buoy bells in the fog. Every evening he would watch the lamplighter ignite the gas lamps on the street corners until the whole city twinkled like a jewel box on the hills overlooking the water.

Since the Frosts moved often, and both parents were teachers, Robbie was tutored at home to supplement his irregular attendance at school. His little sister, Jeanie, two years younger than he was, did not attend school regularly, either. The children liked their mother's method of teaching; she took them for long walks in the sunshine and pointed out objects of interest. They would climb to the top of a hill and watch the ships in the bay, examine the trees, leaves, grass, and flowers, and listen to lectures on history and geography. But their reading lessons tended to be neglected. Their mother loved to recite the romantic poetry of Edgar Allen Poe, Robert Burns, and others aloud. She became very dramatic while doing this, and held the two children spellbound with verse after verse as they sat before her, their eyes shining. She often recited stories from the Bible, as well.

Robbie's father, on the other hand, often went for long periods without seeming to notice the children. He drank heavily, and this sometimes made him mean-tempered. At other times he would suddenly become affectionate and seemed to take pride in his son.

The colorful waterfront town of San Francisco was an exciting place for a boy to grow up. Young Robert Frost loved to watch the sparkling water of the bay and see the cable cars moving up and down the steep hills of the town.

Young Robert Frost spent his chaotic boyhood in the exciting city of San Francisco. He soon learned to love the sea, which he saw every day, shining below the hills and along the rugged coast. But he also learned something of the great and menacing power of the ocean when he was very young. His parents had taken him on a visit to the Cliff House, a restaurant built high on rocks above the crashing surf. It afforded a magnificent view of the turbulent Pacific, and the barking of seals could be heard from rocks jutting out of the water. There was a beach adjacent to the Cliff House, and the youngster was playing on the sand with a long piece of seaweed late one afternoon.

Like many five-year-olds, he wandered away from his parents, completely enchanted by the seashore. Suddenly the sky began to darken, and a storm out at sea whipped up a strong wind and a high tide. Great waves rolled upon the beach, higher and higher, as the wind grew stronger and night began to descend. The youngster imagined himself alone, in danger of being swept away by the ocean. He was terrified and fascinated at the same time. The mighty force of nature was impressed upon him for the first time, and he never forgot it. He ran back to his parents, who thought nothing of the episode. But thirty-six years later, his memory was so vivid that he was inspired to write one of his most famous poems, "Once by the Pacific."

ONCE BY THE PACIFIC

The shattered water made a misty din.
Great waves looked over others coming in,
And thought of doing something to the shore
That water never did to land before.
The clouds were low and hairy in the skies,
Like locks blown forward in the gleam of eyes.
You could not tell, and yet it looked as if
The shore was lucky in being backed by cliff,
The cliff in being backed by continent;
It looked as if a night of dark intent
Was coming, and not only a night, an age.
Someone had better be prepared for rage.
There would be more than ocean-water broken
Before God's last *Put out the Light* was spoken.

Robbie was a sensitive child, but was sturdy, energetic, and loved the outdoors. He worshipped his father, who engaged in such things as six-day footraces and long swims in the cold water of San Francisco Bay to display his manliness. Nothing delighted Robbie more than to be allowed to tag along after his father, whom he was convinced was the strongest, smartest, and bravest man in the world.

His father continued to be active in politics while working as political reporter and editor of several different newspapers. One year he was nominated by the Democratic Party to run for city tax collector, but lost the election. By the time Robbie was ten years old, he was allowed to go with his father to the newspaper office and run errands in the city. He delivered messages and legal documents to City Hall, checked addresses on voter registration lists, and accompanied his father on political campaigns around the city. He beamed with pride whenever his father introduced him to his political friends as "my son, Robert Lee Frost, a true Democrat."

The boy tried to emulate his father's rugged manliness and swashbuckling ways by engaging in contests and trying to outdo other boys. Once he stole a small pig on a dare and sold it to a Chinese storekeeper. Another time he raced a bigger boy twenty laps around

Frost as a boy, above, delivered messages and ran errands for his father, who was campaigning for political office.

the block and won. Robbie first felt the wrath of an irate female when he cheated at playing croquet with a little girl and she hit him over the head with her mallet.

To a boy who so admired his father, it was heartbreaking to go home in the evening and be ignored or rebuffed by his ill-tempered parent. But night after night William Frost would arrive home in a bad mood after drinking and gambling. He would punish Robbie harshly when he misbehaved.

One Halloween the father refused to allow Robbie to make a jack-o'-lantern in the kitchen because, he said, it would make a mess to carve a pumpkin there. All the other neighborhood children had jack-o'-lanterns and were allowed to take them out on the street. Robbie didn't want to go out when he found he wouldn't be allowed to make his.

Suddenly there was a knock at the door, and when Robbie answered it, one of his friends stood there with a freshly carved jack-o'-lantern, lit by a candle.

"It's for you, Robbie," he said. "A surprise, so you can come out with us."

In his despair, Robbie forgot his manners. Before shutting the door in the youngster's face he said bitterly, "My father won't let me have a jack-o'-lantern."

William Frost happened to see this from the living room. He was probably more upset at having his heartless actions known in the neighborhood than by Robbie's lapse in manners. Grabbing a dog chain in the front hall, he beat the boy's bare legs with it until they were bruised and bleeding. Robert Frost never forgot this beating, and he never lost the scars caused by it.

It became obvious to Mrs. Frost that her husband had consumption (tuberculosis) as early as the second year they lived in San Francisco. His racking cough was terrible to hear. At first he refused to believe it was anything more than a temporary ailment. But as time went by, he began to face the fact that he probably had tuberculosis. After any strenuous physical activity the fits of coughing would be especially severe, and the spells grew longer and longer as the years went by. He usually reached for a whiskey bottle to stop the coughing.

Robbie continued to accompany his father as he got sicker and sicker, following him around town, from the newspaper office to political headquarters, saloons, and poolrooms. The boy especially liked to go into saloons where a good free lunch was served with drinks at the bar. While his father gulped down whiskey and schooners of beer to quiet his cough, Robbie would help himself eagerly to slices of salami, crackers, fresh sardines, and the bowl of peeled hard-boiled eggs to be found in every bar. His father paid little attention to him, but generally was not abusive in public. It was at home that the boy continued to fear his father's unpredictable rages. But now the rages were sometimes interrupted by his severe coughing spells, which left him weak and quiet for awhile. Sometimes when they were riding through the streets in a buggy, he would be seized by a fit of coughing and would become so weak that Robbie had to grab the reins and drive the horse himself.

William Frost tried all sorts of cures for his illness, but none of them worked. For a time, he went to a slaughterhouse several days a week and drank the warm blood of pigs and cattle because he had heard it was a cure. Rob used to stand and watch his father force the blood down, grimacing all the while. The year Rob turned eleven, his father became weaker and weaker and the boy began to realize he wasn't going to get better.

On May 5, 1885, the thirty-four-year-old newspaperman lay on his couch in the living room, his breath coming in great, rasping gasps. Belle Frost sat in the next room while a good friend sat with her stricken husband.

The door opened softly and the friend came through.

"Belle, he's gone," he said sadly. "He just died in my arms."

A stricken look crossed Belle Frost's face, but she quickly regained her composure and later told her children that their father would no longer be with them. They wept and wondered, bewildered as they were, what they would do without this dominating, fearsome, and vital personality. Never again would they be filled with terror at the wild rages of their unpredictable, unstable, inconsiderate father; but never again would they be filled with pride at the sight of their strong, handsome, swashbuckling hero.

William Frost had built up more than $20,000 in equities in insurance annuities, but when he knew he was dying he had tried to double the money in the stock market to provide more for his family. He had invested all the money—unwisely—and lost it all. Now the widow had only enough savings to pay for three train fares back to Massachusetts and arrange for shipment of the body. Lawrence, Massachusetts, was their destination, for William Frost, the wandering maverick son, had requested that he be buried with his relatives in the family burial plot.

The forlorn trio made a sorrowful train journey with the black coffin, stopping several times to change trains and have the coffin transferred with them. Throughout the bizarre trip Belle Frost remained composed, comforting the children when they awoke with bad dreams in the middle of the night, as the mournful train whistle echoed through the lonely countryside.

For heartbroken, confused young Robert Frost, the long journey was a turning point.

Isabelle Moodie Frost, Robert Frost's mother, as she looked just before her marriage.

A Student Discovers Poetry

As the funeral procession passed through the gray streets of the mill town of Lawrence, young Rob missed the color, the climate, and the excitement he had known during his life in San Francisco. He took an immediate dislike to New England, and his impression was formed, in part, by the people. He didn't understand the cold, aloof manner of everyone he met, including his own relatives.

His grandparents were very stiff, correct people who felt keenly the tragedy of their brilliant son's wasted life, but would not show it. They did not fully approve of their daughter-in-law and seemed to feel that she could have done more to prevent their son from throwing his life away. They didn't fully accept her explanation that she had been unable to influence him.

Rob soon realized that his grandfather was a very different man from his father. He was *not* bold, reckless, and impetuous; he planned things carefully and was very cautious in money matters. But they had one thing in common that Rob noticed right away: the same cold, ice-blue eyes that seemed to stare right through you. His grandfather was as stubborn and unyielding as his father had been.

Rob, Jeanie, and their mother stayed with his grandparents for awhile after the funeral, while Belle Frost tried to decide what to do for the future. She didn't have enough money to go back to San Francisco, nor any guarantee that she could make a living after she got there. For reasons of her own, perhaps because of her Scottish pride, she decided not to go back to her relatives in Ohio and ask their help. She would raise her children in their father's home area, near his family, whether she was accepted or not.

When Robert Frost's father died, the family brought him back to New England to be buried. Here, the funeral procession has just passed through the quiet, gray-looking mill town of Lawrence, Massachusetts, on its way to the cemetery.

31

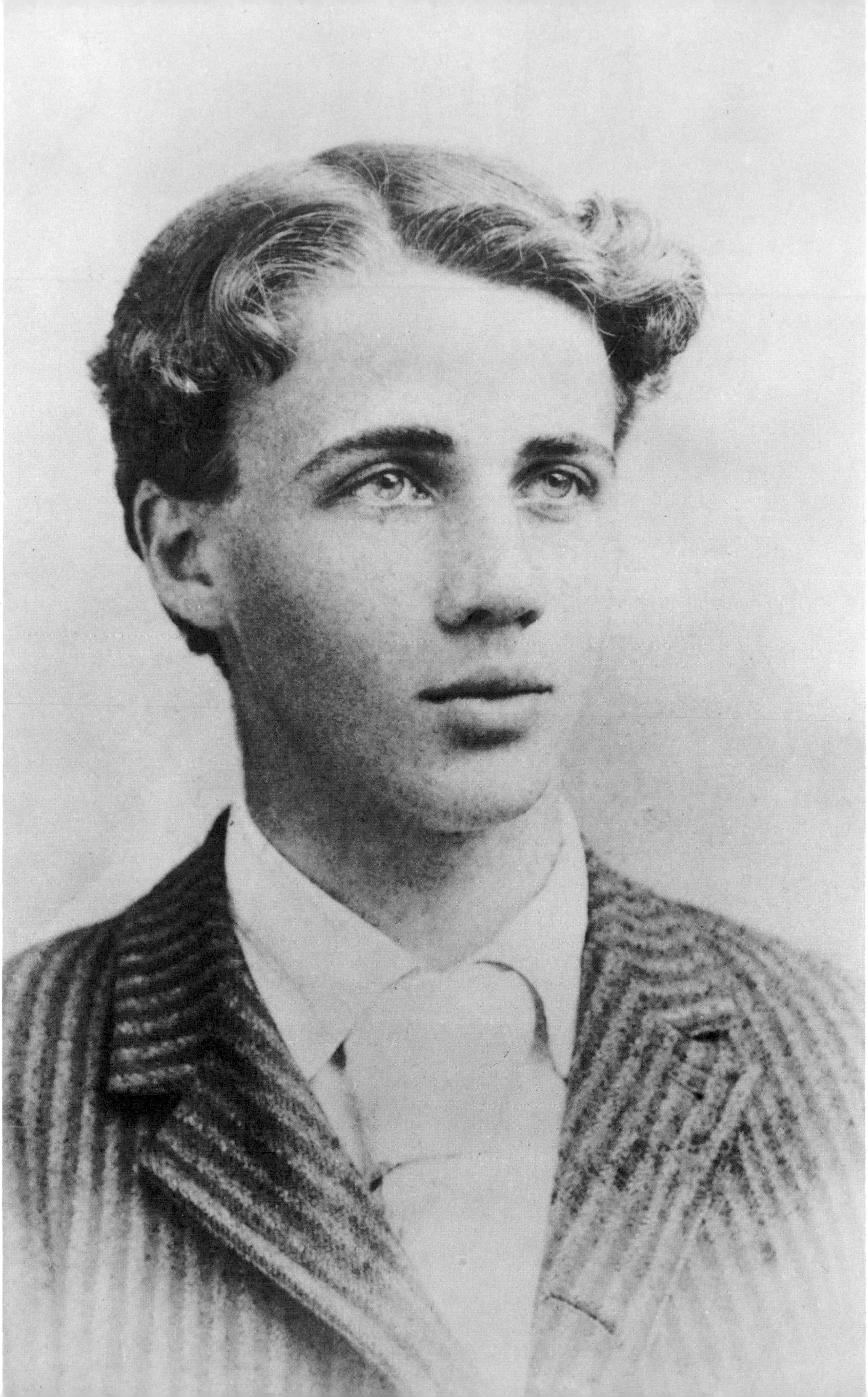

The Jones Library, Amherst, Mass.

For their part, Mr. and Mrs. W.P. Frost, Sr., felt a duty to help their son's widow and his children, but they found them a disturbance to their prim, ordered lives. They were not used to the noise of boisterous children in their big, old-fashioned house. They snapped irritably at Rob and Jeanie for minor offenses and punished them for lapses in formal manners. The youngsters were under strict surveillance all the time.

It didn't take long for Belle Frost to realize that she and her children would have to move out soon to escape the older Frosts' domination. She found a teaching job at Salem, New Hampshire, just over the state line, a few miles from Lawrence, and they moved to a lodging house there.

Because of Rob's lack of formal schooling, he had been assigned to the third grade in a Lawrence school, even though he was eleven years old. But he was transferred to the fifth grade at the Salem school, as a pupil of his mother. He was a lazy, indifferent student, but after two years of studies he began to try harder and was able to pass the high school examinations.

Rob's grandparents wanted him to attend Lawrence High School because it offered a good curriculum. They agreed to pay his train fare between Salem and Lawrence if he would spend time doing chores at their home every afternoon after school. Rob had been working on farms in the summer and after school to help ease his mother's financial burden, so he didn't mind doing more chores to pay his train fare.

From his first day at Lawrence High School, Rob was stimulated by learning and he became an excellent student. One particular teacher aroused his interest in Latin poetry and verse forms and he soon found himself passionately involved in studying this subject. He began to read on beyond each homework assignment, fascinated with the way poetry was constructed.

By the beginning of Rob's senior year he was firmly established as one of two top students in his class. His teachers informed him that he was at the head of his class and was expected to set an example for the other students in his studies. They also mentioned that another student was very close behind in grades, and could overtake him as head of the class if he let down in his studies. This student was a pretty girl named Elinor Miriam White. She had dark, flashing eyes, a proud, sensitive face, and long braided hair.

Far from resenting her as a competitor, Rob was entranced with her after he became acquainted with her in study hall. They talked "on the same wavelength"; she was intelligent enough to understand all the things he liked to discuss. Soon he was walking Elinor home every day before going on to his grandparents' house to do his chores. It became obvious that Rob was "smitten" with this quiet, lovely girl, and people came to think of them as a pair.

This portrait of Robert Frost was taken at the time of his graduation from high school in 1892, when he was eighteen years old.

But Elinor was not as eager to show her affection as Rob, and she made him do the pursuing. She dated no one else, however, from the time Rob first escorted her to an evening function.

They soon discovered that they shared many interests. Their ideals and outlook on life seemed to be similar, although Rob was less practical and more romantic about most things than was Elinor. They both enjoyed poetry and spent much of their time together composing poems and reading and discussing poetry. Rob found poetry a valuable ally in expressing his romantic feelings to Elinor. He would often read aloud from Byron and Shelley.

The first gift Rob gave to his sweetheart was a two-volume set of poems by Edward Rowland Sill, who had recently died as a young man. Some of the verses were romantic, some about death at an early age. They reminded Rob of his own father's premature death.

One day Rob rushed excitedly to Elinor as they met to walk home after school. He was clutching a new volume of poetry he had bought that noon.

"I've discovered one of the best poets I have ever read," he said. "She was from New England and just died a few years ago. Emily Dickinson is her name. You must read this!"

Emily Dickinson's style of plain-spoken, down-to-earth poetry appealed greatly to Rob. It was a refreshing change from the flowery, grand language of most poets. She wrote as people really talked, yet she expressed pro-found ideas and deep feelings. Rob was delighted to find that Elinor admired Miss Dickinson's work as much as he did. Her approach to poetry was later to play a vital role in his own style, and he never ceased admiring it.

Inspired by his father's career, Rob became editor of the school newspaper. He loved to write articles himself, and when he assigned pieces to other students he became irritated when they did a poor job or turned the work in late. Rob was never long on patience, and he finally got so disgusted that he wrote an entire issue himself, then turned in his resignation as editor.

By the time his senior year of high school was drawing to a close, Rob was recognized as the student who would be valedictorian at graduation. Elinor was so close to him in grades, however, that his teachers asked him if he would mind sharing the honor with her as co-valedictorian.

"No, I don't," he quickly replied. And he added gallantly, "if there is any doubt about the honor, I would prefer that she be made valedictorian."

They ended up as co-valedictorians, and each wrote a lengthy address and helped the other rehearse. Their double billing as stars of the ceremonies symbolized to Rob their destiny together. He was sure they would be married. Elinor even looked like a bride in her graduation gown, and he knew he was deeply in love with her. His own relatives were proud of him, and his grandfather said he would pay Rob's expenses

Above, a building on the Dartmouth College campus in Hanover, New Hampshire, where Robert Frost attended school.

at college. The family expected the boy to continue his brilliant scholastic record at a good college.

By now Rob was sure he wanted to be a poet. No other role in life really interested him, but he knew his relatives and friends would consider this a foolish goal. He couldn't make a living doing this, they would tell him. He wasn't even sure he wanted to go to college. After all, he couldn't learn to be a creative poet there, he reasoned. He was disappointed to find that Elinor didn't understand his feelings about it when he discussed it with her. She was positive that it was necessary for both of them to get a college education.

Elinor was to be sent to St. Lawrence, a college in New York State that her parents had selected. Rob was upset that he wouldn't be able to see her except during the holidays, when they would both be at home. But Elinor, more reserved and practical, accepted the coming separation calmly.

Rob had been urged to enroll at Dartmouth College by his grandmother, who didn't want him to attend Harvard College. She had too many burning memories of her son's drinking there many years before. Rob was quickly accepted at Dartmouth on the strength of his good high school record, and after working all summer, he boarded the train to Hanover, New Hampshire, on a September morning. Watching the lovely New England scenery rush by the train window, he wondered what turn his life would take next.

"I've Tasted of Desire"

It was a lonely, confused Robert Frost who became a Dartmouth College freshman in 1892. Since he was a student of proven ability, his relatives expected him to do well at Dartmouth and go on to a respectable career in business or teaching.

The trouble was, he didn't want to do the things everyone expected of him. He knew how important a college education was for a young man going into business or the professions, but this didn't apply to him. He wished sometimes he could change his thinking and have the same goals as other young men, but he couldn't. The most important thing in life to him was poetry, and he wanted desperately to succeed in being a poet. But he was filled with grave doubts about his own ability and he wondered if he would be a failure all his life.

It seemed he had always been a failure with his own relatives. He vividly remembered his father's beatings, his grandfather's coldness toward him, and his grandmother's constant reminders that he wouldn't amount to much if he

---

Frost was unhappy at Dartmouth, where he spent most of his time apart from the other students, who didn't understand his desire to be a poet.

didn't develop better manners, a sense of responsibility, and some practical goals. It seemed that he couldn't please anyone except his mother, who was loyal to him, and Elinor. Even Elinor failed to understand the deep feeling inside him that he must write poetry rather than do anything else.

Rob made only one close friend at Dartmouth—a thin, sickly, intellectual boy named Preston Shirley. They sat up all night and talked about history, politics, religion, and other subjects, and they also played practical jokes and laughed together. But Rob didn't care for the atmosphere of college. He was invited to join a fraternity but after becoming a member, he realized he had little in common with the boisterous, back-slapping extroverts who were his fellow members. He didn't attend their meetings, and they thought him strange —a loner who kept to himself.

Freshmen weren't allowed to take electives, so Rob had no choice in the subjects he studied: Greek, Latin, and mathematics. He really wanted to study literature, and grew bored with his teachers in these other courses.

As the weeks went by, the New England leaves turned to beautiful colors, then faded and fell from the trees. Rob loved most of all to walk alone in the woods surrounding the college campus, the leaves crunching beneath his feet. Here he could think about poetry, his love for Elinor, and his future. He had no idea what that future would be, but he knew he was unhappy at Dartmouth.

One day in the library he discovered a copy of a national magazine called the *Independent*. There was a poem printed

During the fall term at Dartmouth, Frost took many walks alone in the beautiful woods near the campus.

on the front page, and a story about the man who had written the poem. This was the first time Rob realized that poetry magazines existed, and he read the front page several times.

"Someday I'm going to get a poem published in a magazine," he vowed. It was a brave thought, but deep down inside, he wondered if he would ever have the ability. But this was his goal.

From that time on, he thought more and more about being a published writer and less and less about college. He wanted to get away from the unhappy place, and he finally found the excuse he needed. His mother, who was teaching school in Methuen, a town near Lawrence, wrote that she was having trouble with some large bullies in her class. Without even saying good-bye or notifying the faculty, he packed his few

Robert Frost expressed his love of nature in countless poems. In most of these, however, there were deeper meanings. In one of his best-loved poems, "The Road Not Taken," Frost described the need for making a choice between two roads he encountered in a woods. Rather than choosing the well-worn road, he chose to continue his walk on the one less worn by travel. Many readers believe that this decision in the poem referred to Frost's own choice of a way of life. Rather than follow more conventional paths, he chose to pursue a career as a poet, despite the scorn and hardships he knew he would face. This choice was destined to lead Frost to world fame.

THE ROAD NOT TAKEN

Two roads diverged in a yellow wood,
And sorry I could not travel both
And be one traveler, long I stood
And looked down one as far as I could
To where it bent in the undergrowth;

Then took the other, as just as fair,
And having perhaps the better claim,
Because it was grassy and wanted wear;
Though as for that the passing there
Had worn them really about the same,

And both that morning equally lay
In leaves no step had trodden black.
Oh, I kept the first for another day!
Yet knowing how way leads on to way,
I doubted if I should ever come back.

I shall be telling this with a sigh
Somewhere ages and ages hence:
Two roads diverged in a wood, and I—
I took the one less traveled by,
And that has made all the difference.

belongings and quietly left Dartmouth the next day. He had decided to go to Methuen to help his mother. The most cherished thing he took with him was a book of poetry he had bought and read many times.

His mother didn't scold him when he appeared and told her he had left college. He tried to explain his deep feeling for writing poetry, and she sympathized with him. His grandparents were bitter, however, and told him he was a fool.

Rob assisted his mother for the remainder of the school term, and he straightened out the unruly bullies in her school. In this period of history, physical punishment was used to maintain school discipline. Teachers used a rattan switch to give sound whippings to students who refused to obey. Rob took over this task for his mother, and although he wasn't much bigger or older than some of the bullies, he beat them until they stopped defying the teacher and minded their manners in class.

When the school term ended, he took a job as a textile mill worker in Lawrence. Now Elinor joined his relatives, friends, and acquaintances from high school days in saying how disappointed they were in him. It was sad, they said, to see the top student in his class end up as an ordinary laborer.

"What a waste of talent!" they whispered, shaking their heads.

Elinor's mother liked Rob, but her father had little use for a young man with no ambition.

"He'll never amount to anything, fooling around with poetry writing," he said, and he warned Elinor not to go steady with Rob.

For the next couple of years Rob worked in factories and tried his hand as a reporter for a Lawrence newspaper, but his heart wasn't in any of this work. In fact, he was confused about what he should do next to earn a living. He spent much of his time reading and studying every bit of poetry he could find. He also wrote bits of verse and experimented with his own methods of writing. From the very beginning he refused to imitate famous poets; everything he wrote was original. He was too shy to show his writing to anyone except Elinor.

Elinor cared deeply for Rob and believed he really had the talent to become a successful poet someday. But she thought Rob should finish his college education so he would be able to earn a respectable living as a college teacher while writing his poetry. When he talked of marriage, she always put him off, saying she didn't see how he could support her.

He tried desperately to convince her of his talent and to impress her with his poems. But she was involved in

Frost dropped out of college before he finished his fresh-man year. During the next two years he held many jobs, among them that of reporter for a Lawrence newspaper. Here he is shown interview-ing a farmer for the paper.

her college activities and talked about them even when she was home on vacations. Rob was sensitive, and his feelings were easily hurt. He was jealous of St. Lawrence College and the people there who had captured Elinor's interest. His self-confidence sank.

Rob began sending his poems to publishers, thinking he could prove his worth by having them published in magazines. The poem of which he was proudest had been inspired by the sight of a beautiful dead butterfly lying amid some autumn leaves. He tried to express his sorrow at the brief existence of a lovely living thing, and he became aware that this sorrow could also apply to the passing of other beautiful things in life. The words came easily to him as he wrote at the kitchen table, and he didn't stop until he had finished the poem. He knew instinctively that he had a good poem, and that it was his own original style.

Without showing it to anyone, Rob titled the poem "My Butterfly" and mailed it to the *Independent* immediately. It was many weeks before he heard from the editors, but at last he received the thrill of his life—a letter accepting the poem for publication! He would be paid only fifteen dollars, and no publication date had been set, but young Robert Frost was overjoyed.

He decided that the time was ripe to impress Elinor with his ability and make her agree to marry him at last. He planned a master stroke to win her hand. Taking his meager savings, he went to a printer and ordered a volume of five of his best poems printed. It would be titled *Twilight*, and there would be only two copies—one for Elinor and one for him. He chose pebbled leather for a cover and expensive paper for the pages. He was thrilled to see the handsome little books, and he couldn't wait to see Elinor's reaction to this romantic gift. Her letters to him had been cool, but this would change everything.

Soon afterward he boarded the overnight train from Lawrence to her college in New York State. He didn't tell her he was coming, because he was afraid she would be busy with school activities and tell him not to come. Rob's train arrived early in the morning and he made his way to the dormitory where Elinor lived. It was a private house, off campus, where several girls roomed,

Having been treated coolly by the girl he loved, Frost dejectedly leaves the town where she was going to school.

but they were required to obey campus rules. One of the rules stated that they could have no young men visitors except during certain evening hours.

It was a very disgruntled and disturbed Elinor who came to the door. She was annoyed with Rob for visiting her unannounced, and he could see it in her eyes even before she said hello.

"What in the world are you doing here?" she asked.

"I have to talk to you about something that is very important to both of us," he stammered. "I just *have* to talk to you! May I come in for awhile?"

"No! You certainly can't," she said indignantly. "We'll talk when I come home on vacation. You'd better take the next train home to Lawrence."

"Please!" he said, his heart sinking. "I want to give you this . . ."

Before he could stop himself, he handed over his precious book of poems, without the proper little speech he had rehearsed. Elinor took it almost casually, as if she weren't impressed at all. Then she said good-bye and firmly closed the door.

With his head down, Rob walked toward the train station, completely chagrined. He had not even had the chance to show her his copy of *Twilight* and explain that these were the only two copies in the world. In his disappointment and anger, he took his copy out of his pocket and tore it to shreds as he walked along.

He felt as if it were the end of the world, and his feeling didn't change during the days following his arrival in Lawrence. All his self-doubts seemed to rise up again. The object of his love, the one person for whom he tried to write his poetry, had rejected him completely. He wanted to disappear and

never be heard from again. Maybe then she would regret her cruel, hasty action.

Discouraged and hurt, he suddenly packed his bag and caught a train out of Lawrence without telling anyone he was leaving. By that evening he was in New York, where he caught an overnight ship to Norfolk, Virginia. He knew where he wanted to go: the Dismal Swamp—a huge, damp, dangerous wilderness in Virginia. He wanted to wander alone in this swamp, where he might never be found. He would take his chances with death and let his family wonder what had happened to him.

As soon as Rob arrived in Norfolk he asked directions to the Dismal Swamp. He was warned that it wasn't a safe place to walk through, because of snakes, bears, and bobcats. But off he went, trudging for miles through tangled underbrush in the dark of night, the tree branches whipping his face and tearing at his clothes. He was a little frightened, hungry, and tired, but he kept walking, not sure where he wanted to go. Finally he got to the shore of the Dismal Swamp Canal and rode a boat to North Carolina by working as a crewman for a few days. He wandered around, doing odd jobs for food and camping with hoboes on the edge of the forest.

Three weeks later, about the first of December, 1894, he returned home. He admitted to himself that he had been a little silly and immature to run away, but he would admit it to no one else. It had been a real adventure.

His mother was relieved to see him home again, and he was glad to be there. But the happiest sight of all was a copy of the *Independent* lying on a table in his mother's home. On the front page was the poem "My Butterfly," by

---

Unhappy and angry at Elinor's treatment of him, Frost went to Virginia, where he wandered around in the terrifying Dismal Swamp before finally going home about three weeks later

47

Robert Lee Frost. It had been printed the very week he had left Lawrence on his aimless journey. His mother and sister Jeanie were delighted to see his work published in a national magazine, and even his grandfather had to admit that the lazy, irresponsible Rob must have some literary ability.

But more months of odd jobs and stormy scenes with Elinor went by before she finally agreed to marry him. At last he could tell her that he had a means of supporting her. His mother had decided to start a private school, and already had enough students signed up to make it a financial success. She needed two more teachers, and Rob proposed that he and Elinor teach at the school. They could earn enough money to live on, and he would have enough free time to write poetry. Elinor could no longer resist this romantic, unconventional young man, in spite of his temper tantrums, unsteadiness, and impulsiveness. She knew she was taking a chance that she would have to live in poverty, but she believed strongly that he had the talent to be a great poet. And she knew that his love for her inspired him in his writing. Her father was upset and her friends thought she was making a poor choice, but she didn't care.

They were married on December 19, 1895, in one of the schoolrooms where Mrs. Frost taught. Elinor's father refused to attend the ceremony and there were only a few friends present. The lack of an impressive wedding ceremony mattered little. The bride and groom faced an uncertain future without fear.

In December of 1895, Robert Frost and Elinor White were married in the small school run by his mother.

Rural Struggle

Robert Frost and his bride delayed their honeymoon until the end of the school year. Then they decided to spend the summer in a country place in New Hampshire. Carl Burell, a friend from high school days who was working near the village of Allenstown, found a cottage in the country for them to rent.

Carl was interested in plants and flowers, and he loved to putter around a garden. As he helped Rob and Elinor plant flowers and vegetables around the little cottage that summer, his enthusiasm was contagious. A whole new world seemed to open to Rob, and he became fascinated with the details of nature. He had lived in the city, and although he had worked on farms as a laborer, he had never before caught the feeling of being close to nature. This was the beginning of a lifelong passion for country life that would show up in countless poems by Robert Frost in later years.

Rob's poetry efforts weren't very successful during the next couple of years,

and he became discouraged again about his ability. But in September of 1896, he and Elinor became the delighted parents of a baby son, whom they named Elliott. Concerned again about making a steady living, Rob knew he didn't want to go on teaching elementary school. His mother loved teaching children, and his sister Jeanie, who had made a brilliant record in high school, liked it, too. But Rob became bored with teaching elementary subjects.

"Maybe I *should* go back to college and get my degree," he told Elinor one day. "Then I could teach in a college, where it would be more interesting."

Elinor agreed enthusiastically, and her mother rented a small house for them to live in near the college. Rob chose Harvard, and wrote to the dean, giving his full academic record, including the fact that he had dropped out of Dartmouth. He was accepted for admission. His grandfather, with whom he had such an unhappy relationship, sud-

The summer after the Frosts were married, they rented a small cottage in New Hampshire. It was here that Frost's love of country life began.

denly took an interest in Rob again. Grandmother Frost had died, and the stern old man was lonely and perhaps a little more sentimental toward his family than he had been before. Maybe his mixed-up grandson would amount to something after all. He at once offered to pay the tuition at Harvard.

Rob approached his studies at Harvard with more seriousness than he had at Dartmouth, and he compiled an excellent record during his first year. His grades were so good that he won a scholarship for his second year. He didn't take part in campus activities, but hurried home to Elinor and the baby each afternoon. For awhile he took a part-time teaching job to ease the financial burden.

His second year didn't go nearly as well, however. His mother's health was failing and she had difficulty in coping with the problems of her private school. Rob spent quite a bit of his time going back and forth between Cambridge, where Harvard is, and Lawrence, thirty miles away, to help his mother. Worrying about her problems distracted him from his studies. He and Elinor were expecting another baby before the school year would end, and he worried about earning enough money to support their

In 1899, Robert Frost and his growing family spent the summer on a rented chicken farm.

growing family. And he was torn between being a poet and trying to get his degree to become a professor. Could he be a scholarly, regimented faculty member and still be a creative artist? He began to have his doubts.

His nervous tension brought on an illness that became worse and worse. Doctors weren't sure what the ailment was, but they recommended that he leave college and go back to Lawrence and rest. He resigned from school before the first of April, 1899, and prepared to move his family. On April 28, their second baby arrived—a girl, whom they named Lesley.

They spent the summer at a small chicken farm they rented in Methuen. The outdoor life and hard physical work seemed to be just what Rob needed to regain his health. He continued to look after his mother, who was now seriously ill with cancer. It was impossible for her to reopen her school in the fall, and she had to go to a sanitarium in Penacook, New Hampshire.

The following summer, tragedy hit the young family. Their son, Elliott, a happy, healthy little boy, suddenly became ill and died. Their world was plunged into darkness; this was a tragedy they could not learn to accept.

Worst of all, it split Rob and Elinor apart at a time when they should have been especially close to each other. Elinor knew the special grief that only a mother can know when a young child dies. Rob, too, felt grief, but not in quite the same way, and he wasn't able to express his feelings very well. Elinor took this to mean that he really wasn't as deeply hurt as he should be, and she resented the fact. Years later, in a poem called "Home Burial," Rob wrote a very moving account of this inability of a man and woman to communicate.

The attention of well-meaning relatives only made the situation worse in the months that followed. Rob and Elinor both wanted to get away from everything and be by themselves. Finally Elinor took direct action and went to Grandfather Frost. She told him she thought Rob would succeed as a poet, but he needed time to develop and they had to have some way to make a living for themselves. Would he be willing to invest some money to buy them a small farm? Rob's mother had recommended a run-down place of thirty acres in West Derry, New Hampshire, about twelve miles from Lawrence. Rob and Elinor liked the little place the moment they saw it. The old man agreed, but the

In October of 1900, the Frosts moved to this farm in Derry, New Hampshire. It was an ideal place for Rob to settle down and write poetry. The water pump in front of the house was a common sight on farms of that period.

farm would remain his—he would buy it outright and allow them to live there and work it, rather than lend them the money. He told Rob he would give him a year to try to prove himself with poetry, if he would settle down to something else when that failed. Rob didn't agree to this bargain, but his grandfather did purchase the farm.

They moved to West Derry in October, 1900, when the beauty of the New England foilage was at its height. The rolling hills and valleys were ablaze with red, gold, orange, and russet, and the Indian Summer air was clear and mellow, like good apple cider. Farms along the winding country roads were dotted with rows of cornstalks and bright orange pumpkins.

Their little farm was far from fancy— the typical New England house had a side porch shaded by apple trees, bay windows in front, and a shed connecting the house with the barn in back. It was lighted by kerosene lamps with tall glass chimneys, and it was heated by wood-burning stoves—the black kitchen range and one in the parlor. Each had a large wood-box in back of it, filled with stove-length chunks of wood. The wood had to be cut from the surrounding forest, cut again to the proper stove-length, and stored in the woodshed.

A farmer could be reasonably self-sufficient in 1900 if he worked hard enough. He could sell his apple crop, eggs, and milk. He could raise his own vegetables and his wife could can some of them for use the next winter. He could raise, cut, and store his own hay for his horses and cows. His wife could bake the bread and pastry and he could raise pigs for meat. With no fuel, electricity, automobile, or gasoline bills, and with small grocery bills, he had less need for cash than people do today. But he and his wife had to work harder to provide for their own needs.

The peace and quiet of rural life was a perfect atmosphere in which to write poetry. It gave one time to pause and reflect on things. Rob appreciated this, but like many creative people, he didn't like to run his daily life by a set pattern required by a farm. He milked his cow

Rural New England was beautiful when the Frosts moved to Derry, and the apples in their orchard were ripe for picking, eating, and canning.

From *Robert Frost: Life and Talk—Walking*, by Louis Mertins. Copyright 1965 by the University of Oklahoma Press.

at noon and at midnight, rather than early morning and evening as other farmers did. He liked to stay up most of the night, reading and working by the light of the kerosene lamp, then sleep late. His neighbors were early to bed and early to rise, and they thought him a bit strange.

Rob often daydreamed and walked around "with his head in the clouds," and he wasn't a very efficient farmer. He tended to work in spurts rather than plan a day of steady work. When he plowed, the rows often ran crooked. As a result, he wasn't able to earn as much from his farm as most of his neighbors did. But he was happy, for he and Elinor loved the smell of apple blossoms and hayfields in the country air.

Country neighbors often helped each other during the haying season and at other times when more than one man was needed for a job. Rob became fascinated with these strong, proud New England hill folk and their mannerisms. They had a definite code of behavior, born of pride and self-sufficiency. They believed that "good fences make good neighbors," but it wasn't meant in an unfriendly spirit. They believed that a clear dividing line showed each man the limits of his property and his responsibilities. Whatever his neighbor did on his side of the fence was strictly his own business, for New Englanders prized privacy. It was unthinkable to ask a man directly about his affairs.

Rob noticed, too, that actions often took the place of words. If a person needed help, he would get it from his neighbor without much vocal expression at all. The neighbor didn't talk about

---

Robert Frost was fascinated with the New England farmers he came to know when he was living in Derry. Though they often helped each other with farm chores that required more than one man, they respected privacy and never intruded on another's private affairs.

Throughout rural New England there are many low stone walls, built originally by the farmers who settled the land. The stones had been wrenched from the uneven ground and stacked to one side of a farmer's field so that his land could be plowed. The old walls form boundaries between plots of land, and although they are too low to serve any other purpose, they have been preserved.

When Robert Frost lived on his farm near Derry, New Hampshire, he shared one of these stone boundary walls with his neighbor. Each spring the two men worked together to repair the damage done during the long, hard New England winter. Since the wall between their properties served no practical purpose, Frost didn't understand why they should bother to keep it intact. It may have been simply custom, or the New Englander's traditional regard for privacy. The neighbor would say only what his father had said before him: "Good fences make good neighbors." Years later in England, Frost reminisced about the farm and about his former neighbor in his poem, "Mending Wall."

MENDING WALL

Something there is that doesn't love a wall,
That sends the frozen-ground-swell under it,
And spills the upper boulders in the sun;
And makes gaps even two can pass abreast.
The work of hunters is another thing:
I have come after them and made repair
Where they have left not one stone on a stone,
But they would have the rabbit out of hiding,
To please the yelping dogs. The gaps I mean,
No one has seen them made or heard them made,
But at spring mending-time we find them there.
I let my neighbor know beyond the hill;
And on a day we meet to walk the line
And set the wall between us once again.
We keep the wall between us as we go.
To each the boulders that have fallen to each.
And some are loaves and some so nearly balls
We have to use a spell to make them balance:
'Stay where you are until our backs are turned!'
We wear our fingers rough with handling them.
Oh, just another kind of outdoor game,
One on a side. It comes to little more:
There where it is we do not need the wall:
He is all pine and I am apple orchard.
My apple trees will never get across
And eat the cones under his pines. I tell him.
He only says, 'Good fences make good neighbors.'
Spring is the mischief in me, and I wonder
If I could put a notion in his head:
'*Why* do they make good neighbors? Isn't it
Where there are cows? But here there are no cows.
Before I built a wall I'd ask to know
What I was walling in or walling out,
And to whom I was like to give offense.
Something there is that doesn't love a wall,
That wants it down.' I could say 'Elves' to him,
But it's not elves exactly, and I'd rather
He said it for himself. I see him there
Bringing a stone grasped firmly by the top
In each hand, like an old-stone savage armed.
He moves in darkness as it seems to me,
Not of woods only and the shade of trees.
He will not go behind his father's saying,
And he likes having thought of it so well
He says again, 'Good fences make good neighbors.'

it; he just did it, and the other person understood the feeling behind the gesture. Rob also came to admire the sly humor that these people worked into their conversation by the tone of their voices. You had to be quick to catch some of the witticisms that passed back and forth, and he soon learned. It was this type of New England country speech that he worked into so many of his later poems.

Death visited the Frost family again at this point in Rob's life. His mother, Isabelle Moodie Frost, died of cancer at the age of fifty-six, shortly after Rob and Elinor moved to the farm. Rob thought with remorse how little happiness this Scottish-born woman had found in life: her unstable husband had died at thirty-four; her in-laws were unfriendly; she had had to battle to provide for her children; and her only son had shown little progress in the world. Rob wept bitter tears.

He had been on the farm only about a year when his grandfather died. It was an unexpected death, but the old gentleman had taken steps to control his restless grandson's life after he was gone. He had willed the farm to Rob, but on the basis that he had to live there for ten years before it would become his. In this way, he hoped to force Rob to stay settled down long enough to take roots, and perhaps become a good farmer if not a good poet.

Rob continued to write poetry steadily and submit his work to publications, but time and time again it came back marked "rejected." He poured his soul into these poems, and he was deeply hurt when they were so brusquely rejected. Only Elinor could comfort him, by her own faith in his work.

Their family continued to grow; a son named Carol was born in 1902, a daughter, Irma, in 1903, and another daughter, Marjorie, in 1905. Times were hard for the Frosts and they often owed money and had little food in the house. When Elinor's relatives made their rare visits to the farm, they shook their heads and wondered how she put up with this sort of life. They couldn't understand how a former brilliant student like Robert Frost could be content to eke out a bare living on a farm, plowing and doing barnyard chores. They never asked if he were writing poetry, and he never told them.

When their financial plight worsened, Rob got a part-time job teaching English at a local academy. He was so informal and original in his approach to teaching that the students soon found it fun to attend English class. He skipped the textbook approach to grammar and tried to instill in them the love of books. He had the students read stories and poems aloud in class, so they all could participate in the joy of reading.

In 1907, another daughter, Elinor, was born to the Frosts, but she lived only a few days. Again, Rob's wife was plunged into such despair and grief that he couldn't reach her. Again, there was the misunderstanding about his inability to express his own grief. The best he could do was to try to take the other children off her hands. He enjoyed playing with them and loved to take them for long walks, pointing out flowers and birds. He often read aloud to them, to stimulate their interest in books. Elinor never quite got over the deaths of her children Elliott and Elinor, and she and Rob avoided talking about it the rest of their lives.

Rob continued to teach and farm as the years went by, but he didn't feel that he was devoting enough time to poetry. He still had the burning desire to succeed as a poet, even though he was nearing forty and was still a failure.

At times he would think about his life and ask himself, "Am I *ever* going to succeed in life? How much time do I have left?"

But he always supplied his own answer: he *must* succeed. He knew he had learned much over the years and was writing good poetry. Someday he would be recognized for his own original style. He had built up a good-sized collection of poems, some of which had been rejected, some of which had never been sent to magazines.

Finally, more than eleven years after he had first moved to the West Derry farm, Robert Frost did another impulsive thing that was to change his life drastically. While living in Plymouth, where he had gone to teach, he suddenly decided to sell the farm, pack up the family, and move to England. Elinor, in a spirit of adventure, agreed at once. They had never been there and didn't know a soul, but Rob felt he must change his life. Maybe his poetry would be successful in a strange country.

Destiny Calls

Nearly everyone who knew him thought Robert Frost had really gone mad in 1912 when he herded his family onto a ship to England. The Frosts didn't have much money, had few possessions, and weren't sure how they were going to earn enough money to live in England. Rob had some misgivings himself during the long journey, but he didn't tell Elinor or the children about them.

They were quickly settled in a rented country home in England, and one of the first things Rob did was go through his collection of poems, searching for an appropriate group to make a book. He had met a newspaper columnist and asked his advice about publishing companies, and had been told to try David Nutt, a fairly well-known publisher. Since Mr. Nutt had died recently, Rob delivered the package of poems to his widow, saying little about them.

To his great elation, Rob received a card in the mail three days later, saying his book had been accepted! He had been in England only a few days, and had already done what he hadn't been able to do in more than twenty years at home. At last, a book of his poetry was going to be published!

"I think I've reached the turning point at last," he told Elinor.

And he had. The book soon came out under his chosen title, *A Boy's Will*—a phrase from Henry Wadsworth Longfellow's poem, "My Lost Youth." One of the first to review it was Ezra Pound, an already famous American poet who lived in England. Pound praised the book, as did the English reviewers.

". . . it has the tang of the New Hampshire woods," Pound wrote, "and it has just this utter sincerity . . . .This man has the good sense to speak naturally and to paint the thing, the thing

In 1912, Robert Frost and his family took a ship to England, where they were to live until 1915.

From *Robert Frost: Life and Talks—Walking,* by Louis Mertiñs.
Copyright 1965 by the University of Oklahoma Press.

as he sees it. . . . One reads the book for the 'tone,' which is homely, by intent, and pleasing, never doubting that it comes direct from his own life, and that no two lives are the same . . ."

Now Robert Frost was welcomed into the company of famous poets in England, including William Butler Yeats, Henry Newbolt, and W. W. Gibson. Ezra Pound tried to make Frost his protégé and gave him all sorts of advice on writing poetry. But Rob was still too much of an independent New England Yankee to listen to anybody tell him how to write his own poems, no matter how great that person might be. He soon tired of Pound's advice and they stopped seeing each other as often as they had.

One of the things Pound tried to persuade Frost to do was to write free verse, which was just becoming popular with modern poets. Rob liked to write blank verse, which didn't rhyme, but which had carefully metered lines. Free verse not only doesn't rhyme, but doesn't have measured, or metered, lines. Rob remarked that writing free verse is like playing tennis without the net. He felt he could be "modern" in his approach and still write within the framework of traditional poetry.

It wasn't much more than a year later that Robert Frost's second volume of poetry was published in England. His first book of unique, conversational poetry had attracted quite a bit of attention, but the second one, titled *North of Boston*, became a sensation in the literary world. It was made up of many poems he had written during past years when nobody had paid any attention to his poetry. This collection centered on the New England hill-country people that he had known for so long, and it was hailed as a portrait of these unique people that was every bit as honest and fascinating as a painting by Winslow Homer. Rob had been worried about the critics' opinions of the book. He wondered if they would understand the New England he was trying to portray. They did, everywhere.

Edward Thomas, an English reviewer who was to become a close friend of Frost's, praised the book in two of his reviews.

The Frosts enjoyed living in the English countryside. Rob especially enjoyed his friendships with some of the English poets, particularly Edward Thomas. They took long walks in the fields and discussed poetry. The whole Frost family went on day-long picnics.

But 1914 was a fateful year. War broke out in Europe between two groups of nations—Germany and Austria against Russia, France, and Great Britain. It was a new type of war, with tanks, long-range guns, and airplanes being used in battle. German submarines were being used to sink ships in the Atlantic in an effort to stop supplies from reaching England. The United States, under President Woodrow Wilson, was neutral but became alarmed at the actions of the Germans. By February, 1915, Robert and Elinor decided to go home to the United States before the war spread any further. It would be risky crossing the Atlantic, because even neutral ships were under attack by the Germans. But they embarked anyway, and had a routine trip with the children.

The Frosts' large country home in England, Little Iddens (top), was near The Old Nailshop, a lovely house with leaded windows and a thatched roof (bottom).

Robert Frost's love of the rural New England hill country showed in much of his poetry. He wrote of the hot summer sun in hayfields, of the changing color of foliage in autumn, and of the awakening of nature in the spring when flowers, leaves, and grass burst forth into the warm sunshine. But he loved the long, white New England winters, too—the bare birch trees silhouetted against darker evergreens, the crackle of a good fire in a wood stove, the breath of horses visible in the clean, cold air. He enjoyed riding along a winding country road in a sleigh or wagon on days when big snowflakes filled the air, falling silently in deep woods. The beauty and peacefulness of the scene sometimes caused him to stop and admire it. He expressed his feelings in "Stopping by Woods on a Snowy Evening," a poem that is probably known by more people than any other he wrote.

Millions of people have found pleasure in this poem, and in the feeling it conveys. Some are reminded of a similar incident in their past and others are enchanted by the mood, and wish they might experience a feeling like it. President John F. Kennedy often said it was his favorite poem, and Frost was pleased that he liked it. Some people like the symbolism of the last four lines, believing that Frost meant that he enjoyed stopping to contemplate life's meaning (the dark, deep woods) but recognized his responsibilities to work and accomplish something in life. Frost never pointed out exactly what he meant in each line, for he wanted the reader to give his own interpretation to the poem. But the fact that so many different people have received pleasure from various ways of reading the poem is proof of its enduring greatness.

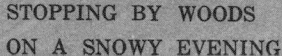

STOPPING BY WOODS
ON A SNOWY EVENING

Whose woods these are I think I know.
His house is in the village though;
He will not see me stopping here
To watch his woods fill up with snow.

My little horse must think it queer
To stop without a farmhouse near
Between the woods and frozen lake
The darkest evening of the year.

He gives his harness bells a shake
To ask if there is some mistake.
The only other sound's the sweep
Of easy wind and downy flake.

The woods are lovely, dark and deep,
But I have promises to keep,
And miles to go before I sleep,
And miles to go before I sleep.

Robert Frost came home a celebrity in the American literary world. Editors and critics wanted to meet him at literary parties—some of them the same ones who had rejected his poems in past years, Rob thought bitterly. Rob dutifully made the rounds of dinners and teas. He listened to publishers, critics, and distinguished poets, including Amy Lowell and E. A. Robinson, praise his work. But as soon as he could, he bought a farm deep in New Hampshire and settled down to write more poetry. This time, however, he wasn't left entirely alone. Letters poured in, writers and professors came to visit him, and he was deluged with invitations to speak and read his poems.

In spite of literary fame, a poet does not become wealthy with the publication of two books. Rob soon found this out, and decided that he really wasn't getting the privacy and solitude he had hoped for on the farm. Since this was the case, he might as well accept an offer to become a professor at a good salary. The offer came from Amherst College, one of the nation's finest small colleges, not far away in Massachusetts. Rob accepted the job with the stipulation that he would be free to devote time to poetry; the college officials agreed. He kept the farm in New Hampshire and spent his summers there in the country he loved so well.

Just before he started his new career as Professor Frost, Rob's third book was published. It was titled *Mountain Interval.* He made it clear that this book was written for Elinor. The lovely poems in it spoke of his love, and of many private memories they had shared through the years. It was a beautiful tribute to his wife, and when Elinor saw the moving dedication, she cried. It remained her favorite of all his books to the end of her life.

The years of heartbreak and failure had not been endured for nothing. Robert Frost's dogged persistence had prepared him for the day when destiny finally knocked. He was ready, and Elinor's faith was justified.

This photograph was taken when Robert Frost returned to the United States from England in 1915. By that time, he was a well-known poet.

Sorrow and Honors

During Robert Frost's first years of teaching at Amherst, America became involved in the First World War. The German sinking of American ships and other acts of war finally resulted in a declaration of war in 1917. A huge army was raised by the draft and volunteers, and soon a million United States troops were on their way to the battle lines in France. The Germans were dug in and so were the British and French, and bloody fighting had only resulted in a stalemate. But with the help of the Americans, the Germans were soon forced to retreat. A young division commander named Douglas MacArthur led his troops with such daring success that he earned a brilliant military reputation —one that would later become even more brilliant. Industrialist Henry Ford, genius of the automobile, turned his huge production plants to the war effort as America's military might surged. And Helen Keller, a blind and deaf woman who had the courage to overcome these obstacles, inspired wounded soldiers by visiting them in hospitals. The Germans admitted defeat and signed an armistice on November 11, 1918.

In 1920, the unpredictable, restless Frost made another one of his lightning decisions: he quit his professor's job and moved back to the New Hampshire farm. There was no particular reason other than his need for a change in routine. His wife and children were used to the impulsive ways of the head of the family, and they didn't object.

Shown here is the farm in Derry, New Hampshire, to which the family returned in 1920 after Frost had left his teaching job at Amherst College.

It was at this time that sorrow again descended on Rob. The cause was his sister Jeanie. The intelligent, sensitive woman had been an ardent pacifist, and she had protested strenuously against the war. As she brooded more and more about the fate of the world, her health —both mental and physical—began to crack. She died without ever seeing Rob again.

Rob continued to shift around as the years went by, teaching at the University of Michigan, Amherst again, and Harvard. Along the way he continued to write poetry, and his worldwide literary reputation grew. He was awarded the Pulitzer Prize for best books of poetry four times—in 1924, for *New Hampshire;* in 1931, for *Collected Poems;* in 1937, for *A Further Range;* and in 1943, for *A Witness Tree.* Frost was the only poet ever to gain that quadruple distinction.

But wherever he taught or traveled to accept awards and give speeches, he could always be found later at one of several New England farms on which he lived. More than ever, he was a man who loved being close to the soil. His deep convictions and quiet strength were never changed by fame and honors, and it showed in his poetry. Other writers, such as Ernest Hemingway,

traveled to various parts of the world in search of adventure and material for novels. But Frost always felt he had more material to write about in his beloved New England hills than he could ever use. He would reminisce about the feelings and pleasures of years gone by and become inspired to write a poem. Remembering how he liked to swing on slender birch trees when he was a boy, he wrote one of his most famous poems, "Birches."

As for his teaching, Frost continued to be unpredictable, informal, and highly individual in his approach. He threw out the textbooks as he had years earlier, and tried to teach his students to love the power of words. He succeeded in most cases. His students enjoyed the tousled-haired professor who ambled into the classroom, sat on the corner of his desk, and swung his legs as if he were sitting on a rail fence. He didn't really lecture, but spoke so informally that it seemed to the class that he was an interesting friend who had dropped by to talk about poetry and books. He kept this same approach through many years—even long after he became the most famous American poet.

Even though Frost periodically complained about the regimentation of teaching, he really enjoyed it. He would

This birch tree on the farm in Derry may have reminded Frost of the trees on which he used to swing when he was a boy.

Among the simple pleasures of life that Robert Frost remembered from his youth were the times he spent swinging to the ground from the tops of young birch trees. In later years, when the complexities of a busy adult world seemed overwhelming, he liked to contemplate this happy pastime. While living in England he became homesick for rural New Hampshire and wrote one of his most famous poems, "Birches."

BIRCHES

When I see birches bend to left and right
Across the lines of straighter darker trees,
I like to think some boy's been swinging them.
But swinging doesn't bend them down to stay
As ice-storms do. Often you must have seen them
Loaded with ice a sunny winter morning
After a rain. They click upon themselves
As the breeze rises, and turn many-colored
As the stir cracks and crazes their enamel.
Soon the sun's warmth makes them shed crystal shells
Shattering and avalanching on the snow-crust—
Such heaps of broken glass to sweep away
You'd think the inner dome of heaven had fallen.
They are dragged to the withered bracken by the load,
And they seem not to break; though once they are bowed
So low for long, they never right themselves:
You may see their trunks arching in the woods
Years afterwards, trailing their leaves on the ground
Like girls on hands and knees that throw their hair
Before them over their heads to dry in the sun.
But I was going to say when Truth broke in
With all her matter-of-fact about the ice-storm
I should prefer to have some boy bend them
As he went out and in to fetch the cows—
Some boy too far from town to learn baseball,
Whose only play was what he found himself,
Summer or winter, and could play alone.
One by one he subdued his father's trees
By riding them down over and over again
Until he took the stiffness out of them,
And not one but hung limp, not one was left
For him to conquer. He learned all there was
To learn about not launching out too soon
And so not carrying the tree away
Clear to the ground. He always kept his poise
To the top branches, climbing carefully
With the same pains you use to fill a cup
Up to the brim, and even above the brim.
Then he flung outward, feet first, with a swish,
Kicking his way down through the air to the ground.
So was I once myself a swinger of birches.
And so I dream of going back to be.
It's when I'm weary of considerations,
And life is too much like a pathless wood
Where your face burns and tickles with the cobwebs
Broken across it, and one eye is weeping
From a twig's having lashed across it open.
I'd like to get away from earth awhile
And then come back to it and begin over.
May no fate willfully misunderstand me
And half grant what I wish and snatch me away
Not to return. Earth's the right place for love:
I don't know where it's likely to go better.
I'd like to go by climbing a birch tree,
And climb black branches up a snow-white trunk
Toward heaven, till the tree could bear no more,
But dipped its top and set me down again.
That would be good both going and coming back.
One could do worse than be a swinger of birches.

Frost's cabin in Vermont was near the Breadloaf School of English, a school for young writers that Frost had helped establish in the 1920's.

suddenly break off from the academic world and go back to the farm to write, but later he would return to teaching.

It was his love of teaching that caused him to help establish the Breadloaf School of English, a special school for young writers, in the early 1920's. It was located at Middlebury College in Vermont, not far from a farm where Frost was to spend many of his later years. The school featured summer sessions called the Breadloaf Writers Conference. Students were chosen for their talent, and many of them were published writers. Here they could exchange ideas, write, and develop their talent by associating with Frost and other famous writers. The school remained one of Frost's favorite projects for the rest of his long life, and it helped set the pattern for other writers' conferences throughout the country.

Robert Frost was awarded many honorary college degrees and other distinctions as his fame increased and the years rolled by. His hard-won fame of the 1920's grew during the depression-haunted 1930's. Times were difficult in the United States and the rest of the world, and millions of people were out of work. Franklin D. Roosevelt became president in 1933, and his administration tried some bold steps to improve the country's economy and help the unemployed. Social Security came into being, to help older people after they retired.

In Europe, dictators named Adolf Hitler and Benito Mussolini headed Germany and Italy, and threatened to make war on other countries. Military leaders had taken over the government of Japan and they, too, threatened to invade other countries. General Douglas MacArthur pleaded for a larger American army to meet these threats, but Congress felt that the country could not afford it.

At home, people tried to forget their cares by watching sports and listening to the happy music called jazz. Babe Ruth, the great home run king, had become a legend in baseball and a hero to millions. Louis Armstrong was the best known jazz musician, and his brilliant trumpet and warm singing ability brought joy to people in all walks of life.

It was ironic that Robert Frost, who had chosen poverty for many years while he struggled to perfect his poetry, should find financial security while so many other people suffered in the depression. The royalties from his books now amounted to a substantial sum.

He used his affluence to help his children, who had problems that he worried about. His son, Carol, idolized him and wanted to be a farmer and poet, too. But he was no more successful as a farmer than his father had been, and he often needed financial help. Carol married and brought Rob and Elinor a grandson named William Prescott Frost —the third in the family to bear that name. Lesley married and had two daughters, but her marriage ended in divorce. Rob gave Irma and her husband a farm, but their marriage, too, broke up in bitterness.

Rob's dreaded memories of his father's fatal tuberculosis came alive again when his daughter Marjorie contracted the illness. Though she recovered from this disease, fate came back to deal a cruel blow. Shortly after she had given birth to a daughter, she was stricken by septicemia, a rare blood infection, and died a slow death at the Mayo Clinic in Minnesota.

To Robert Frost the grief seemed unbearable, but a few years later an even greater darkness and pain enveloped his

life. He and Elinor had taken to spending their winters in Florida to escape the cold weather that always seemed to give Rob the flu. In March of 1938 they were in Gainesville, Florida, and Rob caught the flu anyway. Elinor was nursing him back to health the way she always had when she suddenly dropped dead of a heart attack.

Now Rob was inconsolable; he seemed almost out of his mind with grief. He wished that he might die, too, and he asked himself why fate had taken her just when his fame and fortune were finally established. She had been his inspiration and the mainstay of his life through all the long years of public rejection, poverty, illness, and sorrow.

He could not even bear to talk with his friends during her funeral in Amherst, where he had been teaching recently. He resigned his job, sold the house in which they had been living, and went back to stay in isolation at one of his farms in New Hampshire.

But fate had not finished with him yet. Two years later his son Carol became despondent, considering himself a failure as a poet and in everything else in life. Rob sensed his emotional disturbance and went to him at his farm. He talked to him all one night, and when Carol's mood seemed to improve, he caught a train to Boston in the morning. Two days later he was notified that Carol had shot himself to death.

At this point it seemed as if the whole world were plunged into darkness, too. During the Second World War, much of the world had been devastated and millions of people had been killed. The United States and its allies won a costly victory over Germany, Italy, and Japan after several years of horror.

Rather than succumb to the tragedy that stalked his life, Robert Frost reflected on the meaning and experience of it, and during the following years expressed it through his poetry. He wrote unceasingly, year after year, com-

This photograph of Frost was taken in 1945 in front of the cabin at Breadloaf.

piling some of the great poems that have marked his place in the history of literature.

The ideal love he and Elinor had shared, and his great sorrow at her death, were poured into some of the beautiful, sad verse he wrote. He wrote about love and the many forms it can take, and of the sorrow when it is ended. He described this grief in "The Wind and the Rain," which ends with these lines:

> Rain was the tears adopted by my eyes
> That have none left to stay.

For many years afterward Robert Frost enjoyed the many honors and worldwide fame that he justly deserved. His sage observations and witty remarks at dinners and official functions delighted the press, and the public came to know him better than they knew any other poet. The elderly, white-haired man was accorded great respect even in the Soviet Union, which was engaged in a political struggle with the United States. When Frost visited Russia in 1962, Premier Nikita Khrushchev invited him for a personal visit and they exchanged political views and talked at length about the fate of the world.

Frost the gardener is shown at left in his garden near Breadloaf; right, at home in his study on two different occasions.

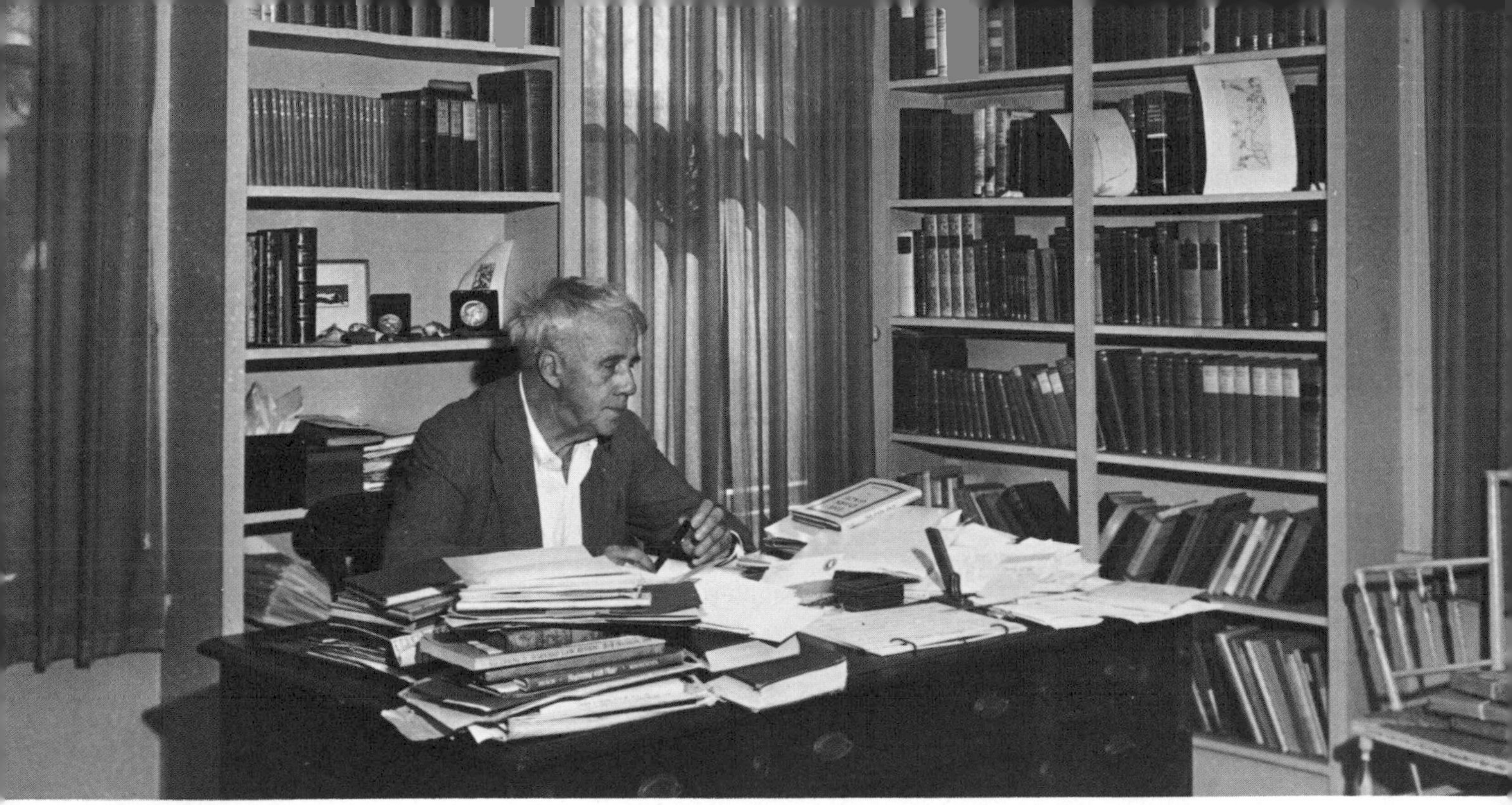

Wide World Photos

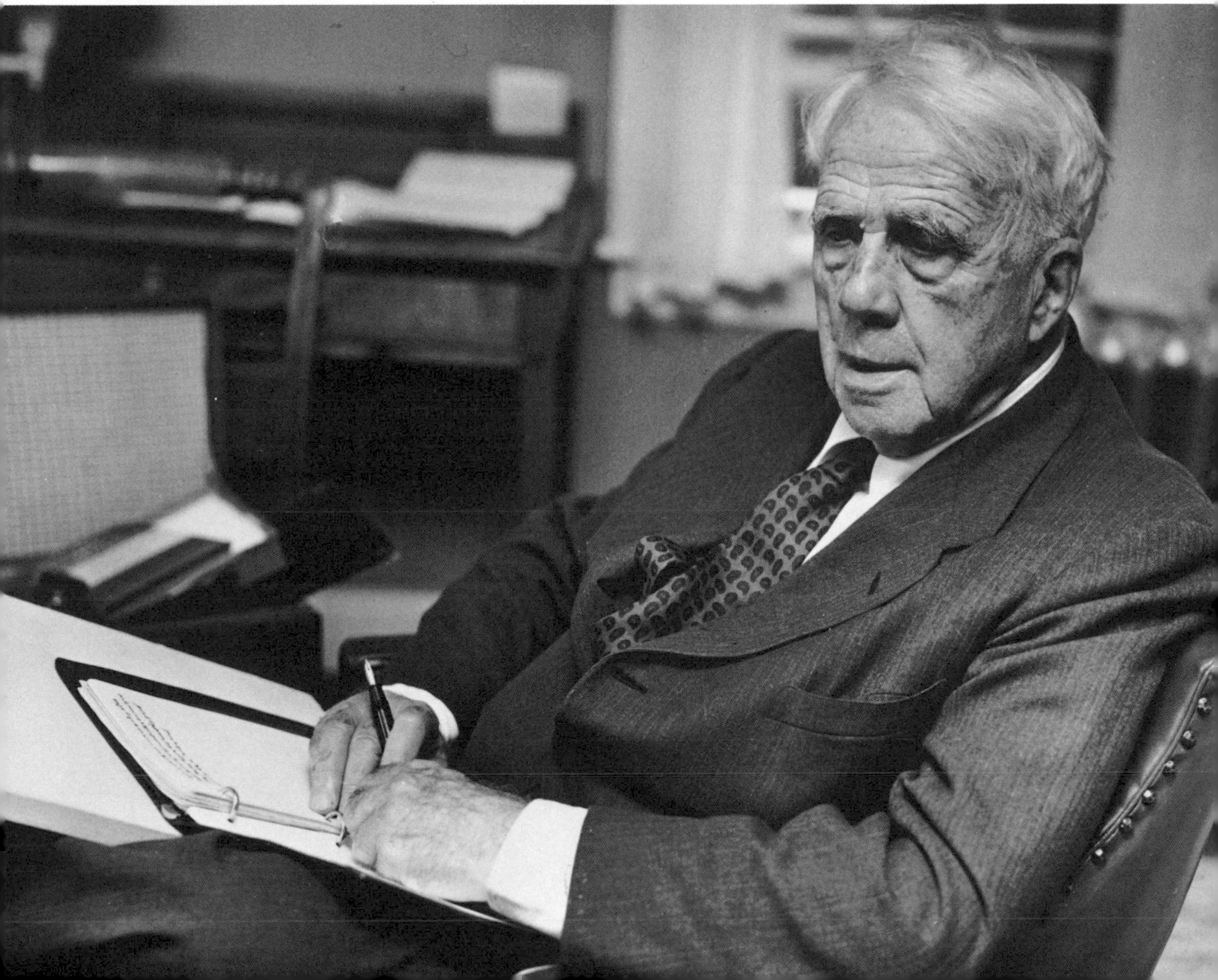

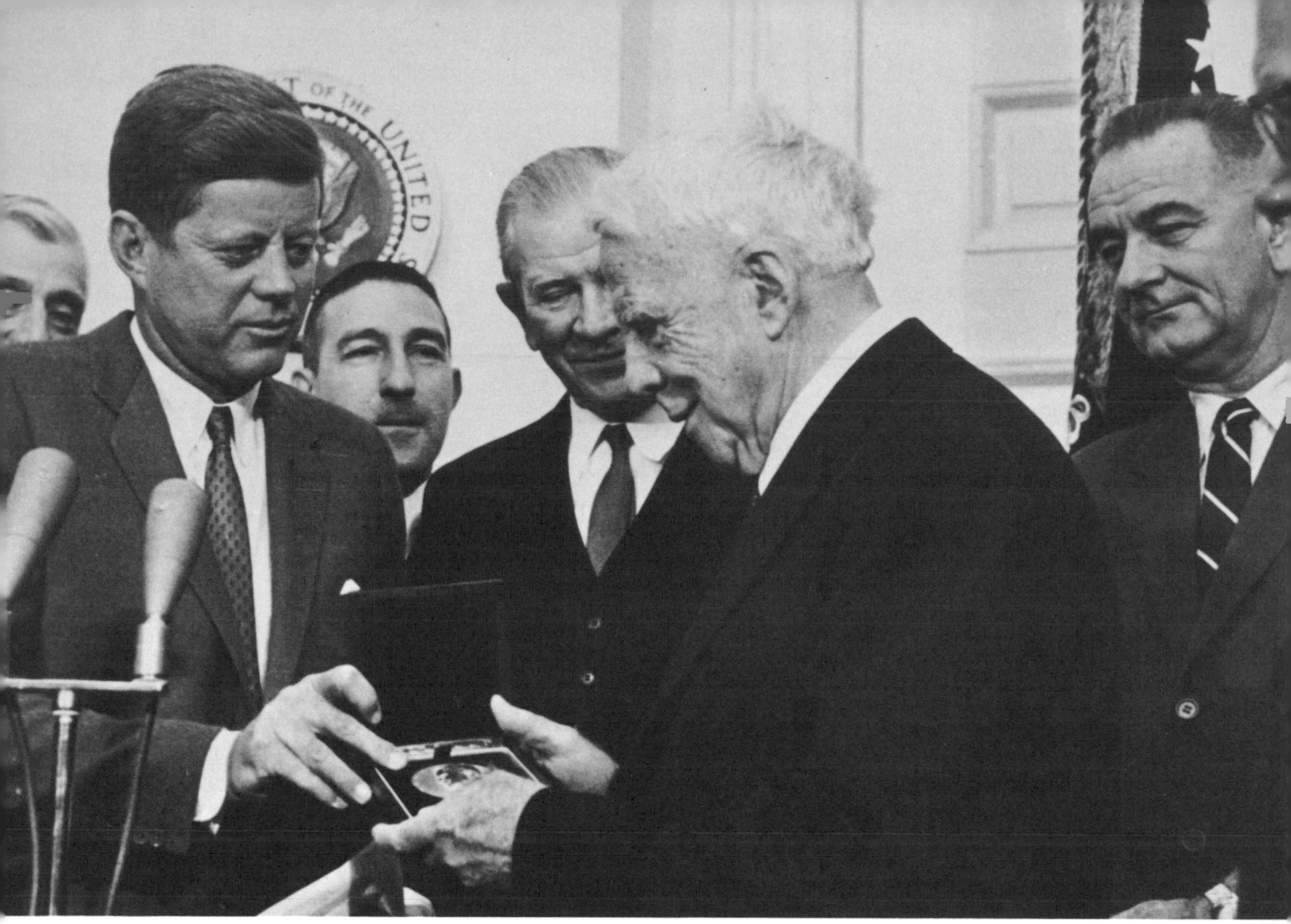

Wide World Photos

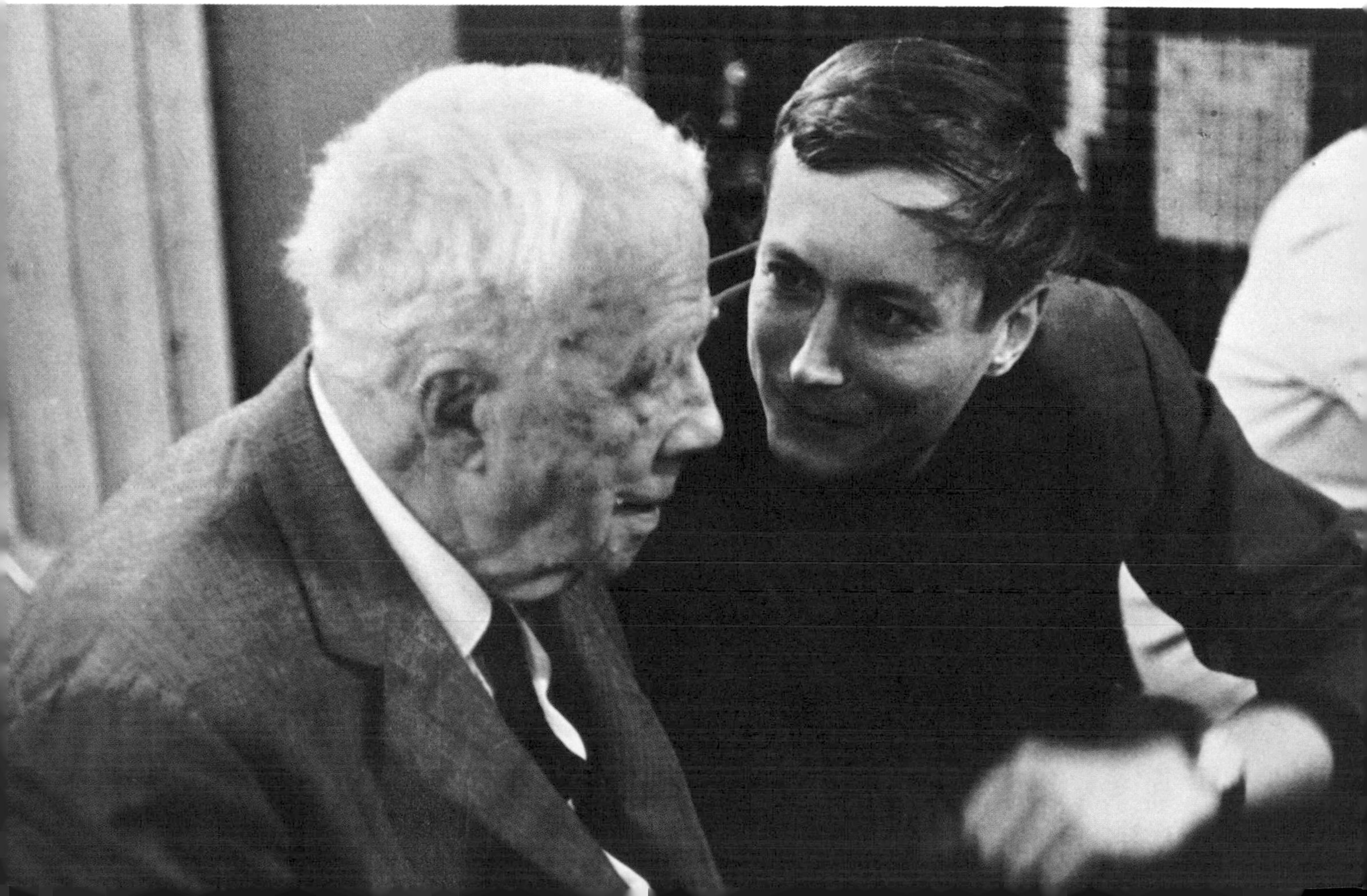

In 1962, President Kennedy presented Frost with a congressional medal for his contribution to American letters. When Frost was in Moscow in 1962, he spoke with the young Russian poet, Yevgeny Yevtuschenko (below left). When Frost traveled to Israel in 1961, he spoke at the Hebrew University in Jerusalem (right).

Wide World Photos

Just a few months after this trip abroad, Robert Frost's long, brilliant life came to a close. He was eighty-eight years old when he underwent a major operation in a Boston hospital. He appeared to be recovering, and was answering some of the hundreds of well-wishers who had written him, when he passed away on January 29, 1963. America knew it had lost one of its rare, great poets, and people from all walks of life paid tribute to him at his funeral services.

He had written his own epitaph in a poem in which he asked that these words be written on his stone: "I had a lover's quarrel with the world." Robert Frost had, indeed, quarreled and struggled with the world, but he never stopped loving it. He left a legacy of poetry that will enrich man's spirit in the ages ahead.

The Johnson Chapel at Amherst College, where memorial services for Robert Frost were held after his death on January 29, 1963.

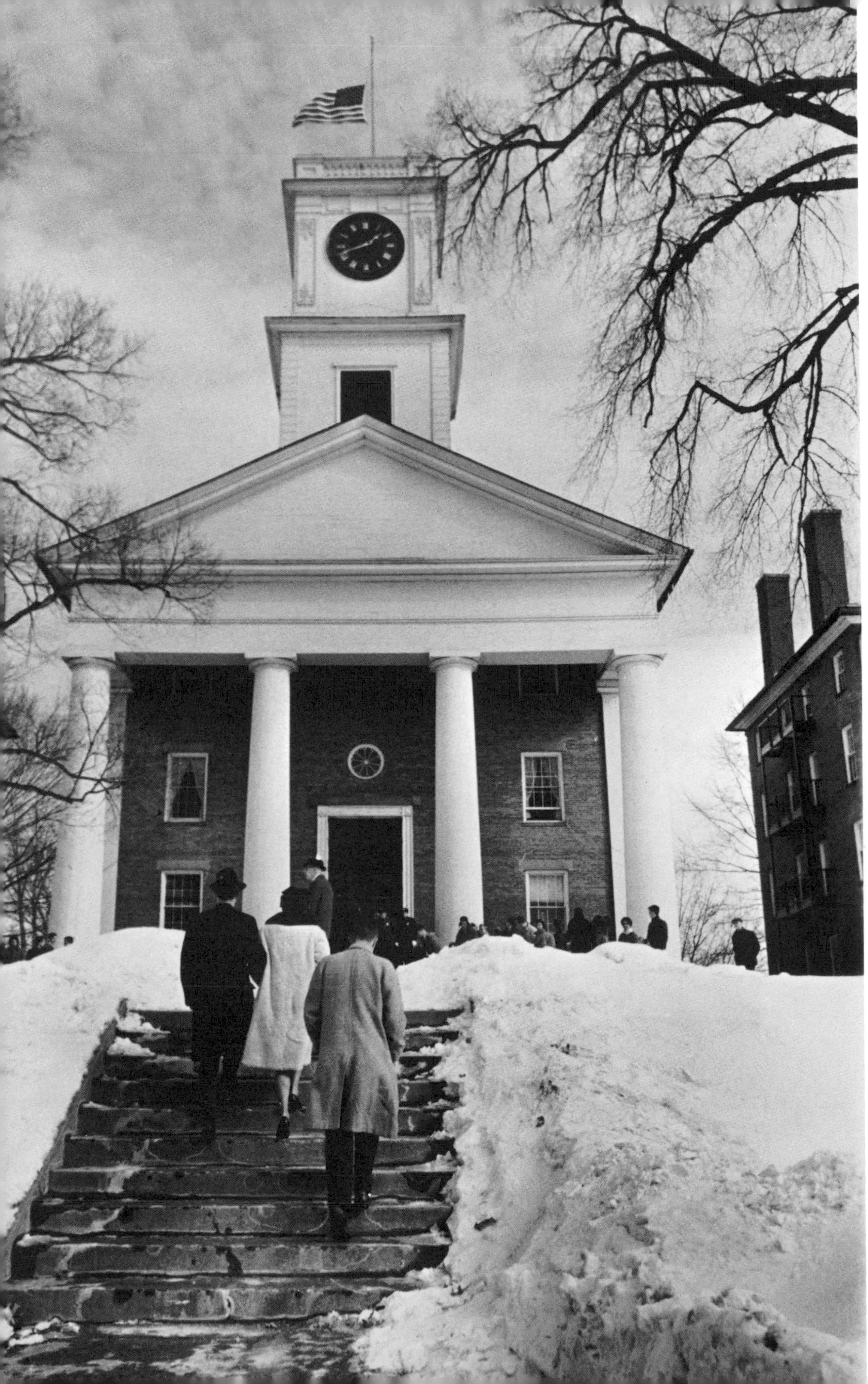

Wide World Photos

Summary

Robert Frost's life demonstrated some truths that apply to those in all walks of life: that success is not easily achieved without hard work and failure along the way, and that belief in oneself can overcome all the doubts and criticisms of others. Many another person would have given up trying to become a poet after many years of failure, but Frost seemed to know his destiny in American literature.

It was an important destiny: to become one of the greatest poets in American history, to win four Pulitzer Prizes, and to become one of the few poets who was admired equally by the literary critics and the general public. He wrote about things that everyone could understand, and he wrote in the plain, unvarnished language of the common man. Yet he wrote with such brilliance and in such an original style that he came to be acknowledged as one of the finest artists ever to represent his country in the field of literature.

Above all, Robert Frost loved humanity and the world, in spite of its imperfections. His poems sang of people and of his love of life. Neither the tragedies nor the disappointments in his life made him a bitter poet, and his words will continue to bring inspiration and happiness to millions of people in centuries to come.

Bibliography

ANDERSON, MARGARET. *Robert Frost and John Bartlett.* New York: Holt, 1963.

BROWER, REUBIN. *The Poetry of Robert Frost.* New York: Oxford University Press, 1963.

BYERS, EDNA. *Robert Frost at Agnes Scott College.* Decatur, Georgia: Agnes Scott College Press, 1963.

COFFIN, ROBERT. *New Poetry of New England.* New York: Russell, 1938.

COOK, REGINALD. *The Dimensions of Robert Frost.* New York: Rinehart, 1958.

COX, JAMES. *Robert Frost, a Collection of Essays.* Englewood, New Jersey: Prentice-Hall, 1962.

COX, SIDNEY. *A Swinger of Birches.* New York: New York University Press, 1957.

DOYLE, JOHN ROBERT. *The Poetry of Robert Frost.* New York: Hafner, 1962.

FROST, ROBERT. *Complete Poems of Robert Frost 1949.* New York: Henry Holt & Company, 1949.

——— . *In the Clearing.* New York: Holt, Rinehart & Winston, 1962.

——— . *Letters of Robert Frost to Louis Untermeyer.* New York: Holt, 1963.

——— . *Masque of Mercy.* New York: Holt, Rinehart & Winston.

——— . *Road Not Taken: An introduction to Robert Frost.* New York: Holt.

——— . *Steeple Bush.* New York: Holt, Rinehart & Winston.

——— . *You Come Too.* New York: Holt, 1959.

GOULD, JEAN. *Robert Frost; The Aim Was Song.* New York: Dodd, Mead, 1964.

GREENBERG, ROBERT, ed. *Robert Frost, An Introduction.* New York: Holt, 1961.

ISAACS, EMILY. *An Introduction to Robert Frost.* Denver, Colorado: Alan Swallow, 1963.

LATHEM, EDWARD, ed. *Interview With Robert Frost.* New York: Holt, Rinehart & Winston, 1966.

LYNEN, JOHN. *The Pastoral Art of Robert Frost.* New Haven, Connecticut: Yale University Press, 1960.

MERTINS, LOUIS. *Robert Frost, Life and Talks—Walking.* Norman, Oklahoma: University of Oklahoma Press, 1965.

MERTINS, MARSHALL. *The Intervals of Robert Frost.* Berkley, California: University of California Press, 1947.

MUNSON, BERT. *Robert Frost; A Study in Sensibility and Good Sense.* New York: Doran, 1927.

NITCHIE, WILSON. *Human Values in the Poetry of Robert Frost.* Durham, North Carolina: Duke University Press, 1960.

REEVE, FRANKLIN D. *Robert Frost in Russia.* Boston: Little, Brown, 1964.

Robert Frost, farm poultryman. Hanover, New Hampshire: Dartmouth Publication, 1963.

SERGEANT, ELIZABETH. *Robert Frost: The Trial by Existence.* New York: Holt, 1960.

SMYTHE, DANIEL. *Robert Frost Speaks.* New York: Twayne, 1964.

SQUIRES, RADCLIFFE. *The Major Themes of Robert Frost.* Ann Arbor: University of Michigan Press, 1963.

SWEENEY, JOHN DAVID. *The Poetry of Robert Frost.* New York: Monarch, 1965.

THORNTON, RICHARD, ed. *Recognition of Robert Frost.* New York: Holt, 1937.

THOMPSON, LAWRANCE. *Fire and Ice; The Art and Thought of Robert Frost.* New York: Holt, 1942.

THOMPSON, LAWRANCE. *Robert Frost.* Minneapolis: University of Minnesota Press, 1959.

——— . *Robert Frost, The Early Years.* New York: Holt, Rinehart & Winston, 1966.

——— , ed. *Selected Letters of Robert Frost.* New York: Holt, Rinehart & Winston, 1964.

UNTERMEYER, LOUIS, ed. *The Letters of Robert Frost to Louis Untermeyer.* New York: Holt, Rinehart & Winston, 1963.

Index

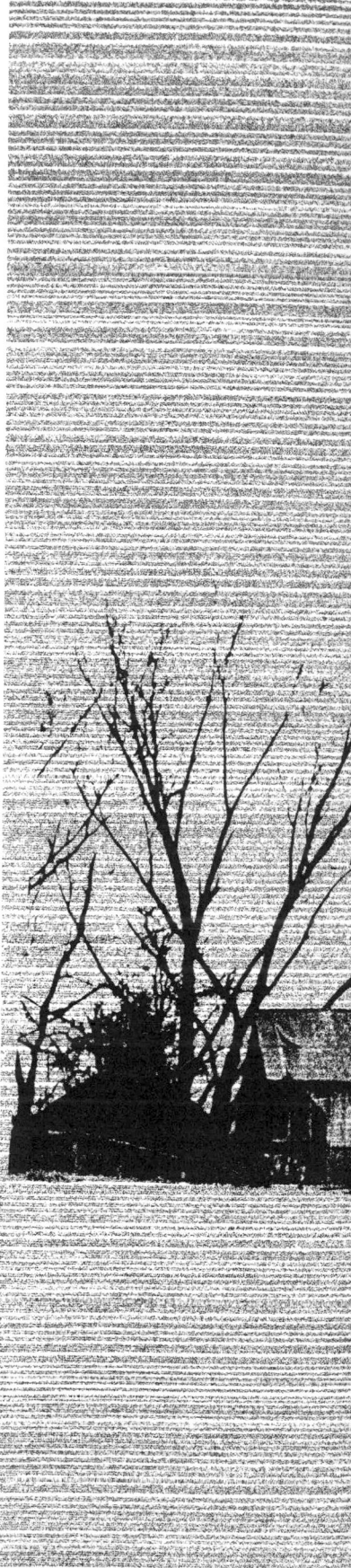

Richards, Norman

Robert Frost